. . . a teacher's guide to accompany

WRITERS
INC

WRITE SOURCE®

GREAT SOURCE EDUCATION GROUP
a Houghton Mifflin Company
Wilmington, Massachusetts
www.greatsource.com

About the
Teacher's Guide

The *Teacher's Guide* will help you use the *Writers INC* handbook effectively in your classroom, and it will also give you many tips and techniques for working with student writers and learners. We have tried to address the questions teachers are asking today in a way that will help you integrate your professional experience with current research.

If you have any questions, please call. (Use our toll-free number—1-800-289-4490.) We are always ready to help or receive feedback.

The Write Source/Great Source Education Group

Written and compiled by
Patrick Sebranek, Dave Kemper, and Verne Meyer
Contributors and consultants: Laura Bachman, Carol Elsholz, Pat Kornelis,
Candyce Norvell, Lester Smith, Vicki Spandel, John Van Rys, Claire Ziffer

Printed in the United States of America

International Standard Book Number: 0-669-47187-9

1 2 3 4 5 6 7 8 9 10 -DBH- 05 04 03 02 01 00

Table of **Contents**

A Quick Tour of the Handbook

Writers INC serves as the perfect language handbook for·high school students. It will help students improve their abilities to write (prewriting through publishing), to think (creatively and logically), and to learn (in the classroom, in small groups, independently). This quick tour highlights the five main sections of the handbook.

1 The Process of Writing

This section helps students understand that writing is a process of exploring and shaping meaning.

"When I write, I am always struck at how magical and unexpected the process turns out to be." —Ralph Fletcher

Writing as a PROCESS

At the start of her career, author Annie Dillard thought that all you really needed was "paper, pen, and a lap" to write something. But before too long, she discovered that "in order to write so much as a sonnet [a 14-line poem], I needed a warehouse." Of course, the author is exaggerating, but only to make a point. Dillard soon learned that she had to spend a lot of time—and write numerous drafts—to produce effective finished products.

You may know from experience what Dillard is talking about. Think of your best essays, reports, and stories. You probably put forth a great deal of effort (enough to fill a warehouse?) to produce each one, changing some parts many times from draft to draft. You may also know that writing really becomes satisfying when it reflects your best efforts. If you work hard at your writing, you—and your readers—will almost always be pleased with the results.

Preview

- Writing Is Discovering
- The Writing Process in Action
- A Closer Look at the Process
- Advice from the Pros

"Good writing excites me and makes life worth living." —Harold Pinter

Traits of EFFECTIVE Writing

When you think of creative writing, you probably think of stories, poems, and plays—forms of writing that require a lot of imagination. This is creative writing in the traditional sense: an inventive, somewhat playful form of writing. And when you think of academic writing, you probably think of essays, reports, and research papers—forms of writing that require a lot of factual information, but not a lot of imagination.

However, it shouldn't be that way. In their own way, essays and reports can be just as creative as stories and poems. Simply put, a creative essay or report exhibits the basic traits found in all good writing: stimulating ideas, clear organization, engaging voice, and so on.

Learning about these traits of good writing—and putting the

Preview

- Quick Guide
- The Traits in Action
- Checklist for Effective Writing

Checklists for the writing process give students a foundation for developing and assessing their own writing.

Checklist for **Effective Writing**

If a piece of writing meets the following standards, it exhibits the traits of effective writing. Check your work using these standards.

Stimulating Ideas

The writing . . .

_____ presents interesting and valuable information.

_____ maintains a clear, specific focus or purpose.

_____ holds the reader's attention (and answers his or her questions about the subject).

Logical Organization

_____ includes a clear beginning, middle, and ending.

_____ contains specific details—arranged in the best order—to support the main ideas.

Engaging Voice

_____ speaks in a sincere, natural way.

_____ shows that the writer really cares about the subject.

Original Word Choice

_____ contains specific, clear words.

_____ presents an appropriate level of language.

Effective Sentence Style

_____ flows smoothly from sentence to sentence.

_____ displays varied sentence beginnings and lengths.

Correct, Accurate Copy

_____ adheres to the rules of grammar, spelling, and punctuation.

_____ follows established formatting guidelines.

2 The Forms of Writing

This section provides students with information, guidelines, and student and professional samples for a wide variety of writing forms—from journal writing to writing an essay of argumentation, from writing poetry to writing a business letter.

145 Personal Writing

Journal-Writing TIPS

There's an old joke about a tourist in New York who asks a cab driver, "How do I get to the Metropolitan Opera House?" And the cabbie replies, "Practice, practice, practice." Old joke . . . great advice. Whether you're involved in music, sports, or writing, you have to practice the necessary skills over and over again.

Journal writing is a great way to practice writing because it is free from the gravitational pull of grades and expectations. You can work on your writing fluency, experiment with different forms, or try out new styles. Listed below are a few tips to get you started.

- **Write nonstop.** Your goal should be to write for at least 10-15 minutes at a time. If you get stuck, write "I'm drawing a blank" until something comes to mind.

- **Focus on ideas.** The real satisfaction in keeping a journal is making new discoveries. Make that your goal.

- **Always date your entries.** And make sure to read them from time to time to see how far you've come.

- **Push an idea as far as you can.** You'll discover new thoughts and feelings when you write about an idea from many different angles. (Keep asking yourself *why* as you write.)

- **Experiment in your writing.** Write like your favorite author or like someone you know. Write in a foreign language or in jazzy street language. Write to make yourself laugh or to give yourself a pep talk. Write using your own rules.

Other Types of Journals

Learning Log @ Writing in a learning log or class journal gets you more actively involved in your course work. It helps you make important facts and ideas part of your own thinking. (See pages 398-399 for more.)

Response Journal @ Writing in a reader-response journal enriches each of your reading experiences—whether you are reading the newest title by your favorite author, an article in a magazine, or a chapter in a class text.

Dialogue Journal @ In a dialogue journal, you and a partner carry on a conversation (first one person writes, then the other) about experiences you have had, books you have read, and issues that concern you.

221

"You are the same today that you'll be five years from now except for two things: the people you meet and the books you read."
—Mac McMillan

Writing a BOOK REVIEW

Everyone has his or her own personal tastes. While you may love Mexican food, your best friend may go for Italian dishes. While you may dig the blues, your brother may like rock or reggae. The same is true of the books you read. While you may enjoy science fiction or science fantasy, the next person may enjoy modern dramas.

One way to share your personal taste in literature is to review the books you read. A book review is a brief essay expressing your personal opinion about a book's value. An effective book review is informative and enjoyable to read. It highlights key parts of a book without giving the whole story away. It provides thoughtful explanations and reflections to support your main points. Most importantly, it helps readers decide if they should read the book themselves.

Preview

- Book Review: Fiction
- Book Review: Nonfiction
- Mini-Reviews
- Assessment Rubric

259

"Adam was the only man who, when he said a good thing, knew that nobody had said it before him."
—Mark Twain

MLA Documentation Style

Most academic disciplines have their own manuals of style for research-paper documentation. The Modern Language Association style manual (*MLA Handbook for Writers of Research Papers*), for example, is widely used in the humanities (literature, philosophy, history, etc.), making it the most popular manual in high school and college writing courses.

This chapter will provide you with guidelines for citing sources according to the MLA style manual. Included is a special section on citing sources from the Internet, including a Web-site address for obtaining updated information. (For complete information about the MLA style, refer to the latest version of the *MLA Handbook*.)

Preview

- Citing Sources: Parenthetical References
- List of Works Cited
- Works-Cited Entries: Books
- Works-Cited Entries: Periodicals
- Works-Cited Entries: Other Sources
- Works-Cited Entries: Electronic Sources

Students learn everything they need to know about conducting research, including writing responsibly and citing sources using MLA and APA style (including Internet sources). A complete sample MLA research paper is also included.

3 The Tools of Learning

Writers INC provides up-to-date guidelines for searching for information, including using the Internet. Important learning skills such as study-reading, vocabulary, speaking, and test taking are covered.

Researching on the Net

One of the best things about the Internet is the wealth of information it makes available. Of course, you have to know how to find that information, how to evaluate it for accuracy, and how to save it for later use.

Locating Information

Your first research task as an Internet user is to find relevant and trustworthy sources of information.

USING AN INTERNET ADDRESS

Sometimes you will have the address of an Internet location, perhaps from a book, a periodical, or a teacher. Type the address into the bar at the top of your browser window; then press the enter or return key. Your browser will send a request for that site across your Internet connection and load it, if it's available.

USING A SEARCH ENGINE

If you don't have any Internet addresses for your topic, a search engine can help you look for sites. (For word-search tips, see page 333.)

Browser Searching Many browsers have an Internet-search function built into them. Just type words about your topic into the address bar, then press "Return" or "Enter," and your browser will supply a list of suggested sites. Select one of those links to load that site.

Web Search Engines The Web offers many different search engines. (See the Write Source site, <thewritesource.com>, for a recommended list.) Some use robot programs to search the Net; others accept recommendations submitted by individuals; most combine these two approaches. When you type a term into a search engine's input box, the search engine scans its listings for matching sites. Then the engine returns recommendations for you to explore. (Most search engine sites also provide topic headings you can explore yourself rather than trusting the engine to do your searching.)

Other Search Engines The Net is more than just the Web. You may find valuable information elsewhere on the Net. These other places have their own search functions. Your favorite Web search engine can lead you to Web pages describing these other services.

CONDUCTING A PAGE SEARCH

To find information quickly within a file, use the available document search functions. Just as your word processor can seek a particular word within a document, most Web browsers can "scan" the text of an Internet document. See your browser's help files to learn how.

Taking the Essay Test

One of the most common (and most challenging) tests in high school is the essay test. There are certain skills or strategies that can help you face this challenge.

Understanding the Question

The first step to handling an essay test effectively is to read the question several times until you are sure you know what the teacher is asking. As you read, pay special attention to the key words found in the question. For example, if you are asked to *contrast* two things, and you *classify* them instead, you have missed the point. Your test score will suffer.

Key Words

Here is list of key terms, along with a definition and an example of how each is used in a typical essay question.

Classify To classify is to place persons or things (especially animals and plants) together in a group because they are alike or similar. In science there is an order that all groups follow when it comes to classifying or categorizing: phylum (or division), class, order, family, genus, species, and variety.

Compare To compare is to use examples to show how things are similar and different, with the greater emphasis on similarities.
Compare the British and American forms of government.

Contrast To contrast is to use examples to show how things are different in one or more important ways.
Contrast the views of the North and South on the issue of states' rights.

Define To define is to give a clear, concise definition or meaning for a term. Defining can involve identifying the class to which an item belongs and telling how it differs from other items in that class.
Define what is meant by the term "filibuster."

Describe To describe is to tell how something looks or to give a general impression of it.
Describe Scout's appearance on the night of the Halloween party.

Diagram To diagram is to explain with lines or pictures—a flowchart, a map, or some other graphic device. Generally, a good diagram will label the important points or parts. (See page 355.)
Diagram our town's government officials according to level of responsibility.

Guidelines for studying and learning help students work with subject matter across the curriculum.

Strategies for Study-Reading

Knowing some of the common patterns of nonfiction makes it easier to understand your assigned reading. Five of these patterns are reviewed in this chapter: *description, chronological order, comparison/contrast, main idea/supporting details,* and *cause and effect.* Knowing these patterns can help you take notes as you read.

Description

Description focuses on sensory details (how something looks, sounds, and feels) to give you a clear picture of the topic. When a selection follows the description pattern, you can use mapping to help you take notes.

Mount Everest, the world's highest mountain at 29,028 feet, towers over the border between Nepal and Tibet. Its Nepali name is *Sagarmatha,* which means "Forehead in the Sky."

Everest is clothed with gigantic glaciers that make their way down its slopes—usually slowly, but sometimes in huge, thundering avalanches of snow and ice that bury entire valleys. Temperatures vary greatly. In January, the average temperature at the summit is -33 degrees Fahrenheit; low temperatures drop to -76°F. The "warmest" month is July, when the average temperature is -2°F.

From June through September, monsoon season brings screaming winds and blinding snowstorms. Winter winds whip around the summit at more than 175 miles per hour—stronger than a Category-5 hurricane.

Mapping

sights
- 29,028 feet high
- gigantic glaciers
- world's highest mountain
- borders Nepal and Tibet
- blinding snowstorms

sounds
- screaming winds
- thundering avalanches

Mount Everest

feelings
- winter cold -76°F
- July average -2°F
- hurricane-strength (175 mph) winds

4 Proofreader's Guide

The Proofreader's Guide—the "Yellow Pages"—provides students with answers to their questions about punctuation, mechanics, usage, parts of speech, and sentence structure. Each part of the Proofreader's Guide contains explanations and examples to illustrate the basic rules.

Helpful charts and lists make it easy to find information throughout the Proofreader's Guide.

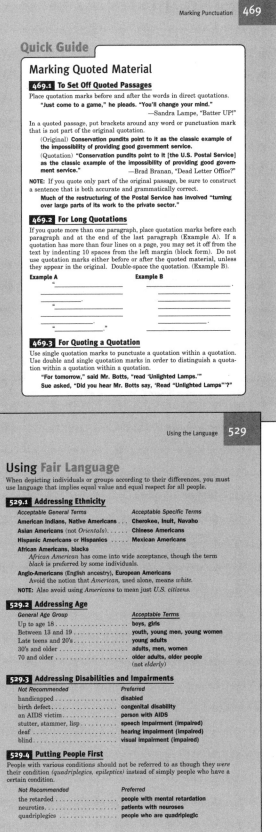

Marking Punctuation 469

Quick Guide

Marking Quoted Material

469.1 To Set Off Quoted Passages

Place quotation marks before and after the words in direct quotations.

"Just come to a game," he pleads. "You'll change your mind."
—Sandra Lampe, "Batter UP!"

In a quoted passage, put brackets around any word or punctuation mark that is not part of the original quotation.

(Original) Conservation pundits point to it as the classic example of the impossibility of providing good government service.

(Quotation) "Conservation pundits point to it [the U.S. Postal Service] as the classic example of the impossibility of providing good government service."
—Brad Branan, "Dead Letter Office?"

NOTE: If you quote only part of the original passage, be sure to construct a sentence that is both accurate and grammatically correct.

Much of the restructuring of the Postal Service has involved "turning over large parts of its work to the private sector."

469.2 For Long Quotations

If you quote more than one paragraph, place quotation marks before each paragraph and at the end of the last paragraph (Example A). If a quotation has more than four lines on a page, you may set it off from the text by indenting 10 spaces from the left margin (block form). Do not use quotation marks either before or after the quoted material, unless they appear in the original. Double-space the quotation. (Example B).

Example A   Example B

469.3 For Quoting a Quotation

Use single quotation marks to punctuate a quotation within a quotation. Use double and single quotation marks in order to distinguish a quotation within a quotation within a quotation.

"For tomorrow," said Mr. Botts, "read 'Unlighted Lamps.'"

Sue asked, "Did you hear Mr. Botts say, 'Read "Unlighted Lamps"'?"

---

528 Using the Language

Agreement of Pronoun and Antecedent

A pronoun must agree in number, person, and gender (sex) with its *antecedent*. (The *antecedent* is the word to which the pronoun refers.)

Cal **brought** his **gerbil to school.** (The antecedent of *his* is *Cal*. Both the pronoun and its antecedent are singular, third person, and masculine; therefore, the pronoun is said to agree with its antecedent.)

528.1 Agreement in Number

Use a **singular pronoun** to refer to such antecedents as *each, either, neither, one, anyone, anybody, everyone, everybody, somebody, another, nobody,* and *a person.*

Neither **of the brothers likes** his **(not** their**) room.**

Use a **plural pronoun** to refer to antecedents joined by *and*; two or more singular antecedents joined by *or* or *nor* are referred to by a **singular pronoun.**

Jared **and** Carlos **are finishing** their **assignments.**

Either Connie **or** Sue **left** her **headset in the library.**

528.2 Agreement in Gender

Use a **masculine** or **feminine pronoun** depending upon the gender of the antecedent.

Is either Connor **or** Grace **bringing** his **or** her **baseball glove?**

When *a person* or *everyone* is used to refer to both sexes or either sex, you will have to choose whether to offer optional pronouns or rewrite the sentence.

A person **should be allowed to pursue** his **or** her **interests.** (optional pronouns)
People **should be allowed to pursue** their **interests.** (rewritten in plural form)

If one of the antecedents joined by *or* or *nor* is singular and one is plural, the pronoun should agree with the nearer antecedent.

Neither **the** manager **nor the** players **were crazy about** their **new uniforms.**

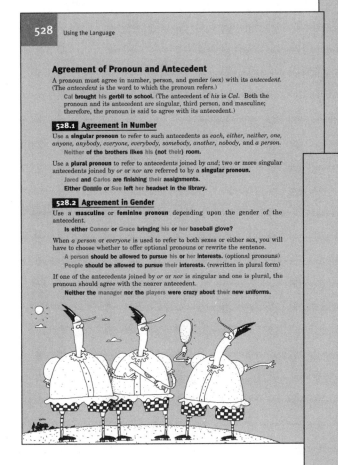

A section about using fair language addresses issues of ethnicity, age, disability, sexism, and matters of appropriate and respectful titles.

Using the Language 529

Using Fair Language

When depicting individuals or groups according to their differences, you must use language that implies equal value and equal respect for all people.

529.1 Addressing Ethnicity

Acceptable General Terms	*Acceptable Specific Terms*
American Indians, Native Americans	Cherokee, Inuit, Navaho
Asian Americans (not *Orientals*)	Chinese Americans
Hispanic Americans or Hispanics	Mexican Americans
African Americans, blacks	

African American has come into wide acceptance, though the term *black* is preferred by some individuals.

Anglo-Americans (English ancestry), European Americans

Avoid the notion that *American*, used alone, means *white*.

NOTE: Also avoid using *Americans* to mean just *U.S. citizens*.

529.2 Addressing Age

General Age Group	*Acceptable Terms*
Up to age 18	boys, girls
Between 13 and 19	youth, young men, young women
Late teens and 20's	young adults
30's and older	adults, men, women
70 and older	older adults, older people (not *elderly*)

529.3 Addressing Disabilities and Impairments

Not Recommended	*Preferred*
handicapped	disabled
birth defect	congenital disability
an AIDS victim	person with AIDS
stutter, stammer, lisp	speech impairment (impaired)
deaf	hearing impairment (impaired)
blind	visual impairment (impaired)

529.4 Putting People First

People with various conditions should not be referred to as though they *were* their condition (*quadriplegics, epileptics*) instead of simply people who have a certain condition.

Not Recommended	*Preferred*
the retarded	people with mental retardation
neurotics	patients with neuroses
quadriplegics	people who are quadriplegic

5 Student Almanac

The Student Almanac helps make *Writers INC* an all-school resource that all students can use in all of their classes.

There are glossaries of math and computer terms.

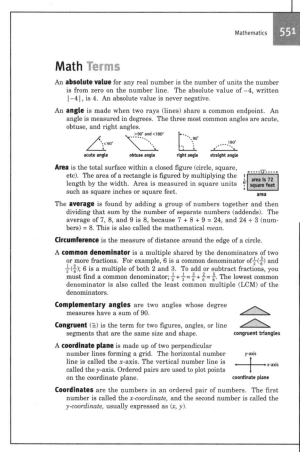

538 Language

6-Year Calendar

Mathematics **551**

Math Terms

An **absolute value** for any real number is the number of units the number is from zero on the number line. The absolute value of −4, written |−4|, is 4. An absolute value is never negative.

An **angle** is made when two rays (lines) share a common endpoint. An angle is measured in degrees. The three most common angles are acute, obtuse, and right angles.

acute angle   **obtuse angle**   **right angle**   **straight angle**

Area is the total surface within a closed figure (circle, square, etc). The area of a rectangle is figured by multiplying the length by the width. Area is measured in square units such as square inches or square feet.

area is 72 square feet

area

The **average** is found by adding a group of numbers together and then dividing that sum by the number of separate numbers (addends). The average of 7, 8, and 9 is 8, because $7 + 8 + 9 = 24$, and $24 \div 3$ (numbers) = 8. This is also called the mathematical *mean*.

Circumference is the measure of distance around the edge of a circle.

A **common denominator** is a multiple shared by the denominators of two or more fractions. For example, 6 is a common denominator of $\frac{1}{2}(\frac{3}{6})$ and $\frac{1}{3}(\frac{2}{6})$; 6 is a multiple of both 2 and 3. To add or subtract fractions, you must find a common denominator; $\frac{1}{2} + \frac{1}{3} = \frac{3}{6} + \frac{2}{6} = \frac{5}{6}$. The lowest common denominator is also called the least common multiple (LCM) of the denominators.

Complementary angles are two angles whose degree measures have a sum of 90.

Congruent (≅) is the term for two figures, angles, or line segments that are the same size and shape.

congruent triangles

A **coordinate plane** is made up of two perpendicular number lines forming a grid. The horizontal number line is called the *x*-axis. The vertical number line is called the *y*-axis. Ordered pairs are used to plot points on the coordinate plane.

y-axis

x-axis

coordinate plane

Coordinates are the numbers in an ordered pair of numbers. The first number is called the *x-coordinate*, and the second number is called the *y-coordinate*, usually expressed as (x, y).

There are useful tables and charts, full-color world maps, and a time line that begins with 1500.

578 History

1500	1520	1540	1560	1580

U.S. & WORLD HISTORY

1492 Columbus reaches the West Indies.

1513 Ponce de León explores Florida; Balboa reaches Pacific.

1519 Magellan begins three-year voyage around the world.

1521 Cortez defeats Aztecs and claims Mexico for Spain.

1559 Spanish colony of Pensacola, Florida, lasts two years.

1565 Spain settles St. Augustine, Florida, first permanent European colony.

1570 League of the Iroquois Nations formed.

1588 England defeats the Spanish Armada and rules the seas.

1597 British Parliament sends criminals to colonies.

SCIENCE & INVENTIONS

1507 Book on surgery is developed.

1509 Watches are invented in Germany.

1530 Bottle corks are invented.

1531 Halley's Comet appears.

1545 French printer Garamond sets first type.

1543 Copernicus's theory proclaims a sun-centered universe.

1558 Magnetic compass invented by John Dee.

1585 Decimals introduced by Dutch mathematicians.

1590 First paper mill is used in England.

1596 Thermometer is invented.

LITERATURE & LIFE

1500 Game of bingo developed.

1503 Pocket handkerchiefs are first used.

1507 Glass mirrors are greatly improved.

1513 Machiavelli's *The Prince* published.

1517 Reformation begins in Europe.

1536 First songbook used in Spain.

1538 Mercator draws map with America on it.

1541 Michelangelo completes largest painting, "The Last Judgment."

1564 First horse-drawn coach used in England.

1580 First water closet designed in Bath, England.

1582 Pope Gregory XIII introduces the calendar still in use today.

1599 Copper coins first made.

U.S. POPULATION: (NATIVE AMERICAN)   **(SPANISH)**

approximately 1,100,000   1,021

Introducing the Handbook

The pages in this section can be used to introduce *Writers INC* to your students and get them on the road to becoming active, independent learners.

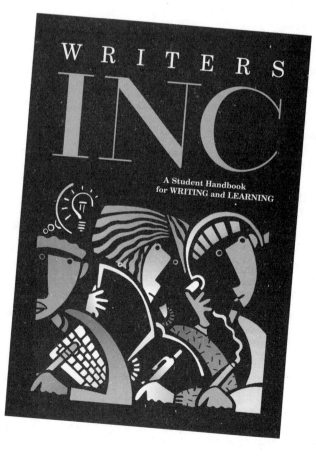

Getting-Started Activities

Writers INC was developed by experienced teachers and writers for students in high school and beyond. More than anything else, we wanted to put together a handbook that students would find helpful and enjoyable to use. Over the past several years, teachers have told us what they do to help their students become efficient handbook users.

Many of their suggestions, plus some of our own, are contained in this section of the *Teacher's Guide.* Here's what you will find:

○ General Start-Up Ideas
○ Your First Week with the Handbook
○ Reproducible Activity Sheets and Answer Keys

Planning Guide

Many of the following suggested start-up activities are incorporated into "Your First Week with the Handbook" on page 9.

Designing Your Own Handbook

Before you even hand out *Writers INC*, ask your students what they would put into an all-purpose handbook if they were in charge of designing one for their school. After students have compiled their lists, go over them in class. Then have students look through a copy of *Writers INC* and locate the ideas from their own lists that have been included in the handbook. Also ask them to start a second list of items in the handbook that they wish they had included in their design.

First Impressions

Give students at least 10 minutes to preview *Writers INC.* Then have them write freely for 10 minutes about their first impressions, or have them complete the reproducible activity sheet on page 10 in this section. Follow with group or class discussions about their discoveries.

Using the Handbook

After students have previewed the handbook, have them complete "Using the Handbook," the activity sheet on page 11. (Discuss page iii in *Writers INC* with the students before they begin their work.) To help students become even more familiar with the handbook, have them complete

one of the searches on pages 12-14 in this guide.

Scavenger Hunts

Once students understand how the handbook works, consider implementing the scavenger hunts on pages 17-18 in this guide. You could also ask students to make up scavenger hunts of their own.

Minilessons

On a regular basis, implement minilessons that get students into the handbook. See pages 111-152 in this guide for ideas.

Pick 'n' Share

Give your students the following assignment: Find one page, one short section, one set of guidelines, one illustration, or one quotation you find interesting, entertaining, stimulating, or valuable. Students should then be prepared to share their discoveries.

Clustering to Learn

After students have previewed the handbook, have them develop a cluster with *Writers INC* as the nucleus word. (If they don't know how to cluster, refer them to the handbook to find out.)

Cubing (Directed Freewriting)

Have students explore their thoughts about *Writers INC* using "Directed Writing," page 46 in the handbook. They should select at least three different modes to explore.

Why Write?

Have students read and react to "Why Write?" on pages 1-2 in the handbook. Then ask them to develop their own "Reasons to Use a Handbook" list. Their lists can be silly, serious, or somewhere in between.

Read and React

Have students read any section (at least 2-4 pages) in the handbook and then write a brief personal reaction to it.

Write Source Web Site

Introduce students to <thewritesource.com> and use the accompanying activity sheet on page 15 in this guide.

Your First Week with the Handbook

The following sequence of activities will help you and your students get to know *Writers INC*. (Adjust to meet your group's needs.)

Day 1

- Pass out copies of *Writers INC*. Give students sufficient time to review their handbooks.
- Have them complete "First Impressions of *Writers INC*," the activity sheet on page 10 in this section.
- Afterward, ask students to share their impressions with a partner or small group. If time permits, discuss *Writers INC* as a class, focusing on the handbook's format, function, surprises, and so on.

Day 2

- Review "Using the Handbook" on page iii of *Writers INC*. Then have students complete "Using the Handbook," the activity sheet on page 11 in this section.
- After discussing the results of the students' work, assign "Pick 'n' Share." (See the previous page.) If time permits, have students begin to share their discoveries with the class.

Day 3

- Have students continue sharing their "Pick 'n' Share" discoveries.
- Then assign one or two of the handbook searches included in this section. (See pages 12-14.) Discuss the results of their work at the end of the class period.
- If you have a computer lab, consider implementing "<thewritesource.com>," page 15.

Day 4

- Have students read and react to "Why Write?" on pages 1-2 in the handbook. Then ask students (in pairs) to develop a "Reasons to Use a Handbook" list. These lists can be serious, silly, or somewhere in between. Have a sharing session at the end of the class period. Also post these lists around the classroom.

Day 5

- Ask students to determine how *Writers INC* can best meet their individual learning needs using "*Writers INC* Planning Guide," the activity sheet on page 16. (Afterward, discuss the results of their work.)
- Introduce some scavenger hunt questions. (See pages 17-18.) If time permits, invite students to create and submit their own questions for future scavenger hunts.

First Impressions of *Writers INC*

Writers INC is a unique handbook for learning. It contains everything students need, from journal-writing ideas to conversion charts; but don't take our word for it. Check out this interesting text for yourself. Page through the handbook from start to finish or, if you wish, from back to front. The choice is yours. Then complete the activity below.

> **Write** freely and honestly for at least 2 or 3 minutes on each of the following topics. Don't stop and think too long about your writing. *Remember:* The title of this activity is "First Impressions." (Use your own paper if you feel that you need more room for your writing.)

Cover (Check out the front and the back covers.)

Format (How is information presented on each page? What types of graphics are used?)

Illustrations (What do they look like, and how are they used?)

Purpose (How would you use *Writers INC*?)

Interesting Extras (Did you find any pleasant surprises?)

Rating (How would you rate this book on a scale from 1 to 10 with 10 being high? Why?)

Using the Handbook

Your handbook is designed to be useful to you not only in English class, but also as a handy reference book in other classes. It is a basic tool for any writing task from preparing a paper for a health course to taking notes in a geography class, from giving a speech in a science class to taking an essay test in a history course.

The **Table of Contents** near the front of your handbook gives you a list of the major divisions and the units found in those divisions.

> **Use** the table of contents in your handbook to help you answer the following questions.

1. On which pages will you find a discussion of the traits of effective writing?

2. Where would you turn for the start of "Writing Persuasive Essays"?

3. On which pages will you find helpful guidelines for writing poetry?

4. Which pages hold a list of literary terms?

5. On which pages will you find guidelines for writing an editorial?

6. Which pages offer information about writing a research paper?

7. Which page would you turn to for information about writing a letter of application?

8. Which pages contain information about creating a multimedia report?

9. Which pages tell you how to mark punctuation?

10. Where does the section on world maps begin?

The **Index** at the back of the handbook is one of its most useful parts. It is similar to the table of contents since it will also help you find things in the handbook. But the index contains much more information. It is arranged in alphabetical order and includes all the important topics discussed in the handbook. Some important topics are highlighted to make them even easier to locate. The numbers after each entry in the index are page numbers.

> **Use** the index at the back of your handbook to help you answer the following questions.

1. Which page will help you correct a sentence fragment?

2. Which page offers a list and description of figures of speech?

3. Which pages will help you write an e-mail message?

4. Which page offers hints for conducting an interview?

5. Which pages discuss writing a speech?

6. Which page explains *biannual* and *semiannual*?

7. Which page has a chart listing the various classes of pronouns?

8. Which page would help you pinpoint a date in the year 2004?

9. Which pages explain common mathematical terms?

10. Which pages provide an explanation of the U.S. Constitution?

Handbook Search A: Locating Information

> **Using** your handbook, answer the following questions.

1. What is *clustering?* ....

....

2. What is an *analogy?* ....

....

3. A comma splice is a mistake made when ....

....

4. What is meant by the term "bandwagon"? ....

....

....

5. According to parliamentary procedure, can a person interrupt a speaker to reconsider

a motion? ....

6. What are the benefits of keeping a learning log? ....

....

7. What is one use of underlining (italics)? ....

....

8. What is the final step in the writing process? ....

9. What does the root word *greg* mean? ....

10. Irony is ....

11. List three transitions or linking expressions that can be used to conclude or
summarize a point you are making in your writing.

....

....

Handbook Search B: **Locating Information**

> **Using** your handbook, answer the following questions.

1. Are commas used to set off restrictive or nonrestrictive clauses? ....
....

2. What is a research paper? ....
....
....

3. How many kilometers are there in a mile? ....

4. What is the past tense of the verb "drag"? .... "bite"? ....

5. Choose the only correctly spelled word from the following: villian, transfered, sincerely,
and sacriligious. ....

6. What are two types of résumés? ....
....

7. On which planet would you weigh the most? ....
....

8. Identify one guideline that you seldom practice for taking an essay test.
....
....

9. In what class would you probably be reading a book with the Dewey decimal system
number 970? ....

10. Which country has the coordinates 15° N, 86° W? ....

11. Which president served two nonconsecutive terms? ....

12. What does the prefix *retro* mean? ....

Handbook Search C: Getting to Know Your Handbook

Using your handbook, find suitable words to complete the chart below. Be sure the words you select begin with the letters in the left-hand column. Use each word only once. *Note:* You won't necessarily find a word that corresponds to each letter for all of the categories.

	Commonly Misspelled Words	Literary and Poetry Terms	Computer and Internet Terms	Prepositions	Commonly Mixed Pairs (Usage)	Countries I Have Never Seen	Information Packages
W							
R							
I							
T							
E							
R							
S							
I							
N							
C							

<thewritesource.com>

> **Bring** up the Write Source Web site <thewritesource.com> on your browser to complete this exercise.

1. Where is the Write Source based? ....
....

2. List two links to publishing sites. ....
....
....

3. List three writing topics for grades 9-12 found on the site.
....
....
....

4. What is the subject of the sample multimedia report for *Writers INC?*
....

5. According to the "Search Engines" page, what are search engines? ....
....
....

6. When citing electronic resources in MLA style, if a Web site has no title, what do you

use in its place? ....

7. Where will you find a link to the Camp Swift Web site? ....

8. What is the e-mail address for the Write Source? ....

9. What is the subject of the sample APA research paper? ....

10. What is one of the sites listed under "Homework Help"? ....
....

Writers INC Planning Guide

Writing, reading, speaking, listening, and thinking are all essential language skills. It's important for you to know that *Writers INC* can help you in all of these areas.

> **Complete** the list below by writing down two or three specific chapters, checklists, or charts and their page numbers in the handbook that would help you become a better writer, reader, thinker, and so on. (Be prepared to explain your choices to your classmates.)

Writing: ....

....

Reading: ....

....

Thinking: ....

....

Speaking: ....

....

Studying: ....

....

....

> **List** your class schedule, excluding your English class, on the back of this sheet. (Leave space between each class.) Identify one or two specific pages, charts, or checklists that would be helpful in each of these classes.

Scavenger Hunts

The scavenger hunts on the following pages provide students with opportunities for using the handbook. By becoming familiar with the contents of the handbook, students will naturally use it more often as each need arises. Continued use will build confidence and help students become more self-reliant as editors and proof-readers of their own writing.

Implementation

There are several ways the scavenger hunts can be used in and out of the classroom. Probably the best way to begin is to simply read one of the questions to your students at some point during class and observe them as they "hunt." You will undoubtedly have to help a number of your students, especially if they aren't in the habit of using an index.

Once a majority of students have found the correct page number and answer, ask them to share this information and—just as importantly—where and how they found it.

After students get the hang of it, scavenger hunts can be used as time permits. For example, you might assign one to be completed for the following day, especially if you plan on discussing that topic. You can also ask students to make up scavenger hunts of their own.

Scavenger Hunt Questions

1. Which trait of effective writing deals with the arrangement of your writing?

2. So what if you've used a cliche? What's wrong with that?

3. A friend is having trouble writing topic sentences. What formula does your handbook suggest that will help?

4. You've been told to write a narrative paragraph. What distinguishes a narrative paragraph from other types of paragraphs?

5. One of the most common methods of organization for your paragraphs is to organize details by time. What are the other ways?

6. Your writing suffers from "primer style." What is this style ailment and what's the cure?

7. Your teacher has told you to select a narrative topic to write about for tomorrow. Where in your handbook will you find writing topics? Which narrative idea would you choose?

8. What is personification? What example is provided in *Writers INC*?

9. According to the postal service's preferred way of addressing a business envelope, which words or abbreviations should be followed by punctuation?

10. In a dictionary, what part of speech is *vi* an abbreviation for?

11. If it's not a new sports car, what is SQ3R?

12. What does the root *arch* mean? What are three words containing this root?

13. Where would you find a sample storyboard for a multimedia report?

14. List two red flags (signals to be suspicious) for any Web site you view.

15. How do you use a semicolon to combine short sentences into longer ones?

16. You would like to become a better speller, but you don't know how. What advice does *Writers INC* offer?

17. Is it correct to write *alot* or *a lot*? Is it correct to write *alright* or *all right*?

18. To avoid sexism, which are the acceptable occupational titles: businessman or executive, chairman or chair, mailman or mail carrier?

19. Is Saturn a terrestrial planet or a Jovian planet? What about Earth?

20. What is the atomic weight of calcium?

21. There are modes of writing such as narrative, expository, etc. What is a *mode* in mathematics?

22. Seattle, Washington, is farther north than Toronto, Canada! What other United States cities are north of Toronto?

23. The 22nd Amendment to the Constitution limits the terms of the U.S. president. What year was it ratified?

24. Who was Ulysses S. Grant's first vice president?

25. In the order of succession to the presidency of the United States, who is fourth in line?

Answer Key

Using the Handbook (page 11)

1.	pages 21-26	**1.**	page 83
2.	page 115	**2.**	page 236
3.	pages 179-184	**3.**	pages 312-313, 334
4.	pages 233-241	**4.**	page 330
5.	pages 188-189	**5.**	pages 424-425
6.	pages 245-254	**6.**	page 492
7.	page 305	**7.**	page 504
8.	pages 433-436	**8.**	page 538
9.	pages 455-474	**9.**	pages 551-556
10.	page 559	**10.**	pages 572-574

Handbook Search A (page 12)

1. Clustering is a prewriting activity that will help a writer select a writing idea. (page 43)
2. An analogy is a comparison of ideas or objects that are completely different but that are alike in one important way. (page 136)
3. two independent clauses are connected with only a comma. (page 84)
4. To bandwagon is to avoid using logic in an argument by appealing to everyone's sense of wanting to belong or be accepted. (page 445)
5. yes (page 537)
6. It gets you more actively involved in your course work. It helps make important facts and ideas a part of your own thinking. (page 145)
7. One use is to indicate foreign words that have not been adopted into the English language. (page 470) Answers will vary.
8. publishing (pages 5-6)
9. herd, group, crowd (page 377)
10. an expression in which the author says one thing but means just the opposite. (page 137)
11. as a result, finally, in conclusion (page 104)

Handbook Search B (page 13)

1. nonrestrictive (page 459)
2. A research paper is a carefully planned essay that shares information or proves a point. (page 245)
3. 1.6093 (page 542)
4. dragged, bit (page 509)
5. sincerely (page 489)
6. chronological and functional (page 320)
7. Jupiter (page 543)
8. Answers will vary. (page 410)
9. history or geography (page 341)
10. Honduras (page 562 or 569)
11. Grover Cleveland (page 575)
12. backward (page 373)

Handbook Search C (page 14)

(Answers will vary.)

W	weird		window	within	waist, waste	Western Samoa	Web pages
R	receipt	refrain	resolution	round	right, rite	Rwanda	radio
I	incredible	iambic	Internet	inside	its, it's	India	interviews
T	their	theme	terminal	toward	than, then	Taiwan	television
E	eighth	empathy	e-mail	except	effect, affect	Estonia	encyclopedias
R	reign	realism	RAM	regarding	real, very, really	Romania	records
S	seize	satire	scanner	since	scene, seen	Syria	surveys
I	inquiry	imagery	interactive	into	infer, imply	Ireland	indexes
N	niece	narrator	network	near	new, knew	Nicaragua	newspapers
C	conscious	comedy	crash	concerning	coarse, course	Columbia	catalogs

<thewritesource.com> (page 15)

1. Burlington, Wisconsin
2. *Merlyn's Pen, Writes of Passage, Kid's Space, Kid News, Midlink Magazine*
3. Answers will vary.
4. Social Security funds, importance of saving now

5. They are on-line services that allow you to search for sites and files on the Internet.
6. Use a descriptive term such as "Home page" without an underscore.
7. Other Links
8. contact@thewritesource.com
9. social loafing
10. Star Tribune's Homework Help, Homework Central, Mr. Megaw's Homework Page

Writers INC Planning Guide (page 16)
(Answers will vary.)

Writing
Proofreader's Guide (pages 455-531)
Chapters:
A Guide to Prewriting (pages 41-52)
A Guide to Drafting (pages 53-58)
Rubrics—Expository Essay (page 114), Research Writing (page 284)

Reading
Chapters:
Using the Library (pages 337-349)
Reading Graphics (pages 351-356)
Study-Reading Skills (357-366)
Improving Vocabulary Skills (pages 367-381)

Thinking
Student Almanac (pages 533-587)
Chapters:
Thinking Skills (pages 437-446)
Writing to Learn (pages 397-404)
Improving Classroom Skills (pages 383-388)

Speaking
Chapters:
Speech Skills (pages 421-432)
Multimedia Reports (pages 433-436)

Studying
Chapters:
Test-Taking Skills (pages 405-419)
Listening and Note-Taking Skills (pages 389-396)
Writing to Learn (pages 397-404)

Scavenger Hunts (pages 17-18)

1. logical organization (page 26)
2. A cliche is an overused word or phrase that bores the reader. (page 88)
3. An interesting subject + a specific feeling or feature about the subject = an effective topic sentence. (page 96)
4. A narrative paragraph tells a story of one kind or another. (page 98)
5. order of location, illustration, climax, compare/contrast, cause/effect, problem/solution, definition or classification (page 52 or pages 100-103)
6. Ailment: Primer style is a style with many short sentences, one right after another. Cure: Do some careful sentence combining. (page 132)
7. Page 135 (Topics will vary.)
8. Personification is a figure of speech in which a nonhuman thing is given human characteristics. (page 138 or 236) *"the pale moon . . . stared"*
9. No punctuation is used in the new system. (page 307)
10. intransitive verb (page 346)
11. a technique for study-reading: Survey, Question, Read, Recite, Review (page 364)
12. Arch means "chief," "first," "rule." Examples will vary. (page 375)
13. page 436
14. The site is anonymous, information is one-sided, etc. (page 453)
15. You join two or more closely related independent clauses that are not connected with a coordinating conjunction. (page 461.4)
16. Be patient, check the correct pronunciation, check the meaning and history, . . . (page 490)
17. a lot; all right (pages 491-492)
18. executive, chair, mail carrier (page 530)
19. Saturn is a Jovian planet; Earth is a terrestrial planet. (page 543)
20. 40.08 (page 544)
21. number or item occurring most frequently in a list of data (page 553)
22. Anchorage, AK; Nome, AK; Spokane, WA; Duluth, MN; etc. (page 561)
23. 1951 (page 574)
24. Schuyler Colfax (page 575)
25. secretary of state (page 576)

Using the Handbook in the Classroom

Using the *Writers INC Handbook* in the Language Arts Classroom

Q. Can teachers develop a language program with *Writers INC* and the *Teacher's Guide?*

A. Most definitely. These two resources can serve as the foundation for a language arts program promoting, among other things, student-centered learning, writing as a process of discovery, and the reading-writing connection. These products can also serve as the foundation for a schoolwide writing and learning program. (See pages 63-76.)

Q. How should teachers plan a program with these two resources?

A. Since *Writers INC* functions mainly as a writing handbook, that is where teachers should first focus their attention. Two very basic questions should be answered during initial planning: **How will writing instruction be approached?** Will students engage in writing workshops? Will writing be integrated into core units? **What types of writing will be covered?** Will personal forms of writing be emphasized in grade 9? Will expository essays be of primary importance in grades 10 and 11, and persuasive essays in grade 12?

"Approaches to Writing," pages 53-62 in this guide, will help teachers answer the first question. Teachers can answer the second question by reviewing the forms of writing covered in the handbook. (Teachers should also refer to the framework of writing activities for grades 9-12 listed on page 23 in this guide.)

Q. What about the language arts?

A. Teachers will find major sections in the handbook related to searching, reading, and thinking skills.

Searching for Information (pages 323-349)
Various primary and secondary sources can be emphasized at different grade levels. In addition, students can explore the Internet and the library in more depth from year to year.

Reading Skills (pages 351-381)
A number of different patterns of nonfiction should be practiced at each grade level. We also suggest that the glossary of prefixes, suffixes, and roots should be the focus of vocabulary study. (See 107-108 in this guide for help.)

Thinking Skills (pages 437-446)
This section addresses thinking from a number of different perspectives. The primary focus of attention in one grade might be recalling and understanding information; in another grade, applying and analyzing information; and so on.

Q. What about study skills?

A. In "Study Skills" (handbook pages 383-419), teachers will find a variety of guidelines related to studying and learning. Perhaps classroom skills could be emphasized in one grade, listening and note taking in the next grade, and test taking in the following grade.

Q. What else should teachers remember when planning with *Writers INC*?

A. Teachers should always remember to turn to the "Introductory Notes" in the *Teacher's Guide* (pages 34-52) whenever they are planning a unit around a particular chapter in the handbook.

What specific types of writing are covered in *Writers INC*?

This chart lists a possible sequence of activities, moving from personal writing to more inventive and reflective writing. Use this framework when planning a high school program with the handbook. The types of writing in italics are covered in the *Writers INC Program Guide*.

9	10	11	12
PERSONAL WRITING			
Personal Narrative (Memory)	Memory of a Person	Memory of School Life	Extended Personal Narrative
Related Memories	"Unpeopled" Memory	Memory of a Group	Personal Essay
SUBJECT WRITING			
Description (Person)	Description (Place)	Profile of a Person	*Case Study*
Interview Report	Eyewitness Account	*Historical Profile*	*Venture Report*
CREATIVE WRITING			
Memory Poem	Poetry About a Person	Found Poetry	Statement Through Poetry
Fictionalized Journal Entry	Patterned Fiction	Fictionalized Imitation	Genre Writing
Dialogue Writing	*Monologue Writing*	*Ad Script*	Play Script
PERSUASIVE WRITING			
Persuasive Paragraph	Persuasive Essay	Essay of Opposing Ideas	*Position Paper*
Pet Peeve	Editorial	Personal Commentary	Essay of Argumentation
ACADEMIC WRITING			
Expository Paragraph	Expository Essay	Cause/Effect Essay	Essay of Evaluation
Essay to Explain a Process	Essay to Compare	Essay of Definition	Problem/Solution Analysis
WRITING ABOUT LITERATURE			
Personal Response	Book Review	Limited Literary Analysis	Extended Literary Analysis
RESEARCH WRITING			
Summary Writing	Précis Writing	Paraphrasing	*Abstract Writing*
Research Report	Research Paper	Research Paper	Research Paper
WORKPLACE WRITING			
Request Letter	Complaint Letter	Persuasive Letter	Application Letter
Memo/E-Mail	Instructions	Proposals	Résumés

How are the modes of writing covered in *Writers INC*?

Many English curriculums approach writing according to the different modes of writing: *narrative, descriptive, expository,* and *persuasive.* The chart below shows how the modes of writing are covered in *Writers INC.* Teachers may find this chart helpful when planning writing assignments. (The page numbers listed below are for the *Writers INC* handbook.)

NARRATIVE
Narrative Paragraphs   **98**
Sharing a Story   **101**
Writing Personal Narratives   **147-151**
Writing Personal Essays   **152-153**
Story Writing   **168-173**
Playwriting   **174-177**

DESCRIPTIVE
Descriptive Paragraphs   **97**
Order of Location: Paragraph   **100**
Descriptive Writing   **156-157**
Eyewitness Account   **158-159**
Interview Report   **160-162**
Profile of a Person   **163-165**

EXPOSITORY
Expository Paragraphs   **97**
Classification Paragraph   **100**
Explaining a Process Paragraph   **101**
Essay to Explain a Process   **200-201**
Essay of Comparison   **202-204**
Cause/Effect Essay   **205-207**
Essay of Definition   **208-209**
Problem/Solution Essay   **210-212**
Writing Summaries   **403-404**

PERSUASIVE
Persuasive Paragraphs   **98**
Writing Persuasive Essays   **115-122**
Pet Peeve   **186-187**
Editorial   **188-189**
Personal Commentary   **190-191**
Essay of Opposing Ideas   **192-194**
Essay of Argumentation   **195-197**

Using the Handbook as an All-School Writing and Learning Guide

Because a wide range of information is covered in the *Writers INC* handbook, it can be used in many different ways. For example, in many schools the handbook serves as an all-school resource—one that students refer to in every class for help with their writing, study-reading, note taking, test taking, and so on. Once teachers in all subject areas become familiar with the contents of the handbook, they will understand its potential as a writing and learning tool. The following list demonstrates the handbook's cross-curricular value.

Special Note: See pages 63-76 in this guide for more information about writing across the curriculum.

Writing Skills

- Why Write? (1-2)
- Writing as a Process (3-8)
- One Writer's Process (9-20)
- Writing with a Computer (27-32)
- Using Graphic Organizers (48-49)
- Writing Paragraphs (95-104)
- Writing Expository Essays (105-114)
- Writing Persuasive Essays (115-123)
- Academic Writing (199-213)
- Writing a Book Review (221-226)
- Writing Business Letters (297-308)
- Special Forms of Workplace Writing (309-321)
- Guidelines for Thinking and Writing (438)
- Writing to Learn (397-404)
- Reviewing Videos (450-451)

Researching Skills

- MLA Documentation Style (259-274)
- APA Documentation Style (285-295)
- Writing the Research Paper (245-254)
- Writing Responsibly (255-258)
- Types of Information (323-330)
- Using the Internet (331-336)
- Using the Library (337-349)
- Writing a Summary (403-404)

Reading and Speaking Skills

- Reading Graphics (351-356)
- Study-Reading Skills (357-366)
- Improving Vocabulary Skills (367-381)
- Speech Skills (421-432)
- Multimedia Reports (433-436)

Study Skills

- Viewing Skills (447-453)
- Group Skills (384-386)
- Planning Skills (387)
- Completing Assignments (388)
- Listening and Note-Taking Skills (389-396)
- Test-Taking Skills (405-419)

Helpful Charts and Lists

- Language Families (534-535)
- Common Parliamentary Procedures (537)
- Periodic Table of the Elements (544)
- The Metric System (541)
- Math Terms (551-556)
- Maps (557-570)
- Government (571-576)
- Historical Time Line (577-587)

Using the Handbook for Standards-Based Instruction

Today, teachers are expected to use standards to inform instruction. Standards are the tools used to justify and document what is being taught and what students are achieving. As you will see on the next five pages, *Writers INC* can serve as an important resource for planning instruction that meets the essential *writing standards* as developed at the national, state, and/or local level. (The performance standards that follow reflect the writing skills and forms that students should understand and employ in grades 9-12.)

The Process of Writing

Understanding How Writing Works

The student is expected to . . .	*Handbook Pages*
• **use** prewriting strategies, such as freewriting and clustering, to generate and collect ideas for writing.	41-52
• **use** appropriate reference materials and resources as needed during the writing process.	47, 323-330, 331-336, 337-349
• **pay** careful attention to purpose and audience when developing writing.	50, 62, 67, 72, 139, 140
• **establish** a central idea (*topic sentence, focus or thesis statement*), collect details, and organize supporting information for writing.	51, 96, 248-249
• **apply** different methods of support, including paraphrases, quotations, anecdotes, descriptions, sensory details, etc.	56-57, 99, 136-140, 256-257, 258
• **revise** selected drafts by adding, deleting, and rearranging copy—striving for effective content, logical organization, and appropriate voice.	6, 14-15, 59-68
• **edit** drafts to ensure smooth-reading sentences, effective word choice, and clear and accurate copy.	6, 16-19, 75-79
• **use** available technology to support aspects of prewriting, drafting, revising, editing, and publishing texts.	27-32, 33-39

Evaluating Written Work

The student is expected to . . .	*Handbook Pages*
• **assess** writing according to the traits of effective writing.	21-26, 63-67
• **respond** in constructive ways to others' writing.	69-74
• **use** published examples as models for writing.	21-26, 92-93, 196-197, 225
• **review** a collection of his or her own writing to determine its strengths and weaknesses and to set goals as a writer.	26, 35

The Forms of Writing

Writing to Share

The student is expected to develop . . .   *Handbook Pages*

- **personal narratives** that . . .   98, 101, 147-151
  - focus on specific experiences.
  - develop three key elements: characterization, setting, and
    action.
  - begin in the middle of the action, focus on the essential details,
    and end right after the most important narrative moment.
  - reveal the significance of, or the writer's attitude about, the subject.

- **expository compositions** that . . .   97, 100, 102-103,
  - engage the interest of the reader and state a clear focus.   105-114, 199-213
  - elaborate on the focus with supportive details.
  - follow an organizational pattern appropriate to the form.
  - conclude with a summary linked to the purpose of the
    composition.

- **persuasive compositions** that . . .   98, 115-123,
  - state a clear position or focus.   185-189, 195-198
  - include relevant and organized support.
  - differentiate between fact and opinion.
  - anticipate and address readers' concerns and counterarguments.

- **reflective compositions** that . . .   152-154, 190-194
  - examine the importance of personal experiences and events.
  - establish an effective balance between the description of the
    experience or event and the reflective details.
  - come to conclusions that reveal a greater understanding
    of the experience or event, or about life in general.

- **research reports and papers** that . . .   245-295, 323-349
  - originate with an important, relevant subject.
  - focus on a specific part or main idea about the subject.
  - present a clear and organized discussion or argument.
  - use a variety of primary and secondary sources.
  - support the focus or thesis with facts, specific details, and examples
    from multiple sources.
  - provide clear and accurate documentation.

- **fictional narratives** that . . .   167-178
  - develop an effective story line that builds in suspense.
  - use sensory details and effective word choice to develop
    the key elements (characterization, plot, setting, and theme).
  - include a meaningful problem that influences the main character
    and moves the story along.
  - employ a range of narrative strategies (*dialogue,
    foreshadowing, suspense-building actions,* etc.).

Writing to Share (continued)

The student is expected to develop . . .	*Handbook Pages*
• **poems** that . . . - describe, express, and/or reflect upon the importance of a subject. - display an understanding of poetic techniques and a creative use of language.	179-184
• **summaries** that . . . - highlight the main idea and significant details in a reading selection. - reflect a clear understanding of the selection.	401, 402-404
• **responses to literature** that . . . - develop interpretations that exhibit a careful reading and understanding of the literary work. - take a point of view and support it with textual references. - display a personal connection with the literary work.	215-243
• **business and technical forms** that . . . - are purposeful and address a specific audience. - follow the conventions and style for the respective form.	297-308, 309-321
• **multimedia presentations** that . . . - combine text, images, and sound from a number of different media. - use each medium effectively.	433-436

Writing to Learn

The student is expected to . . .	*Handbook Pages*
• **write to learn** in all subjects in the following ways: - keeping dialogue journals - using learning logs - writing response journals - making lists - summarizing or paraphrasing what is heard or read - connecting knowledge within and across the disciplines - synthesizing information	144-146, 397-404, 443

The Mechanics of Writing

Research

The student is expected to . . .   *Handbook Pages*

• **organize** prior knowledge about a topic using a graphic organizer or some other prewriting strategy.	46-49
• **generate** questions to direct research.	47, 251
• **use** various reference materials such as the dictionary, encyclopedia, almanac, thesaurus, atlas, and on-line information as an aid to writing.	332-333, 343-349
• **use** print and electronic sources to locate books and articles.	323-336, 337-342
• **understand** and use tables of contents, chapter and section headings, glossaries, indexes, and appendices to locate information in reference books.	349
• **take** notes from sources such as guest speakers, periodicals, books, on-line sites, and so on.	250, 392-396
• **summarize** and organize ideas gained from multiple sources.	251, 257, 402-404
• **evaluate** the research and frame new questions for further investigation.	246, 251
• **follow** accepted formats for writing research papers, including documenting sources.	252-254, 259-263, 275-288
• **give** credit for quotations and information in a bibliography (*works-cited page*).	264-274, 283, 289-295

Grammar and Usage

The student is expected to . . .   *Handbook Pages*

• **employ** standard English—including correct subject-verb agreement, pronoun-antecedent agreement, verb forms, and so on—to communicate clearly and effectively in writing.	507-512, 526-528
• **understand** the different parts of speech.	501-517
• **write** in complete sentences (and eliminate sentence errors in writing).	81-90, 518-521
• **vary** the types of sentences in writing (*simple, compound, complex*).	522-523
• **use** conjunctions to connect ideas meaningfully.	91, 104, 516

Grammar and Usage (continued)

The student is expected to . . .	Handbook Pages
• **make** writing precise and vivid using action verbs, specific nouns, and colorful modifiers.	130-131
• **learn** vocabulary-building strategies.	367-381
• **correctly use** commonly misused words.	491-500

Punctuation, Capitalization, and Spelling

The student is expected to . . .	Handbook Pages
• **use** correct punctuation and capitalization in writing.	455-474, 475-477
• **spell** accurately in final drafts, including frequently misspelled words, contractions, plurals, and homophones.	472, 478-479, 484-490, 491-500
• **spell** derivatives correctly.	371-381, 484
• **use** syllable constructions and syllable boundary patterns to spell correctly.	346-347
• **understand** the influence of other languages and cultures on the spelling of English words.	534-535

The *Writers INC Language Program*

There are four main components in the *Writers INC Language Program:* (1) the *Writers INC Handbook;* (2) the *Writers INC Teacher's Guide;* (3) the *Writers INC Program Guides* for each grade level, 9-12; and (4) the *Writers INC SkillsBooks* of activities for each grade level, 9-12. Here's how the different components can work in your classroom:

The ***Writers INC Handbook . . .***
serves as the student's core resource
for writing and learning.

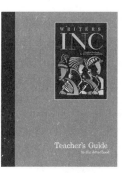

The ***Writers INC Teacher's Guide . . .***
provides basic planning ideas, start-up activities,
and minilessons for using the handbook.

The ***Writers INC Program Guides . . .***
(one for each grade level, 9-12) provide
everything you need to implement the
language program, including teacher's notes
and daily lesson plans, reproducible writing
units, assessment guidelines and rubrics,
and reproducible SkillsBook activities—all
in one ring binder.

The ***Writers INC SkillsBooks . . .***
(one for each grade level, 9-12) offer
students opportunities to practice the
editing and proofreading skills presented in
the *Writers INC* handbook. Pretests and
posttests are included for each section in
the SkillsBooks.

Section-by-Section Teacher's Notes

INFORMATION

Section-by-Section Teacher's Notes

The **Process** of Writing

> ### UNDERSTANDING THE WRITING PROCESS
>
> **Overview:** The opening chapters discuss the importance of writing and provide an overview of the five steps in the writing process—prewriting, writing the first draft, revising, editing and proofreading, and publishing. This recursive process is then modeled in "One Writer's Process," from a prewriting cluster to the final copy. The traits chapter examines the six traits of good writing—stimulating ideas, logical organization, engaging voice, original word choice, effective sentence style, and correct copy. Checklists and rubrics based on these traits appear throughout the handbook. Finally, chapters on writing with a computer and on publishing discuss technology's contribution to the writing process, from editing on-screen to publishing on-line.

WHY Write?

(See *Writers INC Handbook* pages 1-2.)

Major Concepts

- **In school and in the workplace, people write for many practical reasons.** (page 1)
- **Personal writing helps students figure things out, connect with other people, improve their performance in school, get ready for the next step, and shape a meaningful life.** (page 2)

"Why Write?" explains why writing is a valuable, lifelong learning skill. Discuss "Writing is the most powerful means of discovery accessible to all of us throughout life." Review "Reasons to Write" to help students understand the importance of writing and to encourage them to develop their writing skills.

> Students are expected to . . .
> - gain an appreciation of writing as a meaning-making process.

Writing as a PROCESS

(See *Writers INC Handbook* pages 3-8.)

Major Concepts

- **The best writing springs from discoveries made during the process of writing.** (page 4)
- **How a student approaches a writing project depends on the assignment and on the student's writing personality.** (page 4)
- **Producing an effective finished piece of writing requires planning, drafting, revising, and editing and proofreading.** (pages 5-6)
- **A close look at the process will help students appreciate the power of writing.** (page 7)
- **Students gain valuable insights into the writing process shared by professional writers.** (page 8)

This chapter approaches writing as a process of exploration and discovery rather than simply as an end product. The text explains each step in the writing process and offers tips and insights into the craft of writing.

> Students are expected to . . .
> - approach writing as a process to help them meet all of their writing challenges.

ONE WRITER'S Process

(See *Writers INC Handbook* pages 9-20.)

Major Concepts

- **Breaking writing down into steps helps keep a writer on track.** (page 9)
- **Planning before writing is essential.** (page 10)
- **The goal of a first draft is to get all the ideas on paper, without worrying about every word and comma being right.** (pages 12-13)
- **Revising and editing are two different steps; revising focuses on content and organization, and editing focuses on style and mechanics.** (pages 14-19)
- **A basic form of publishing is sharing a finished piece with classmates.** (page 20)

Each step in the process is modeled, from prewriting to publishing. Along the way, some of the complexity and the "messiness" of the process is demonstrated, with words and ideas being cut or moved and new material added as the writer improves and refines his or her work.

Students are expected to . . .
- do the necessary prewriting, drafting, revising, and editing to produce an effective piece of writing.

Traits of
EFFECTIVE Writing
(See *Writers INC Handbook* pages 21-26.)

Major Concepts
- **Effective writing has specific features, or traits, that can be identified and described.** (page 22)
- **Good literature models the key traits of effective writing.** (pages 23-25)
- **Students who know the traits can use them to identify strengths—or weaknesses—in their own writing and in others' writing.** (page 26)

Even the best writers can make their writing stronger by understanding and recognizing specific traits of effective writing. This chapter introduces six traits of effective writing: stimulating ideas, logical organization, engaging voice, original word choice, effective sentence style, and correct, accurate copy. Each trait is defined and modeled to show quality writing in action.

Students are expected to . . .
- assess writing according to specific standards.
- analyze published examples as writing models.
- review collections of their own written work to determine strengths and weaknesses and to set goals as writers.

Writing with a
COMPUTER
(See *Writers INC Handbook* pages 27-32.)

Major Concepts
- **There is an upside and a downside to using a computer for each step in the writing process.** (pages 28-29)
- **Good page design helps make a text clear and easy to follow.** (pages 30-31)

This chapter explores the impact of computer technology on the writing process. The text presents the advantages and disadvantages of using a computer during each step of the writing process. Typography, spacing, and graphic devices are discussed as elements of effective page design.

Students are expected to . . .
- use available technology to support aspects of prewriting, drafting, revising, editing, and publishing texts.

PUBLISHING
Your Writing
(See *Writers INC Handbook* pages 33-39.)

Major Concepts
- **There are many ways to publish writing.** (page 34)
- **Portfolios, collections of writing, showcase students' skills and progress.** (page 35)
- **Good writers don't publish a work until it is truly ready.** (page 36)
- **The Internet offers many publishing opportunities.** (pages 38-39)

This chapter thoroughly examines publishing, the final step in the writing process. It offers publishing ideas, tips for preparing a portfolio, suggested places to publish, guidelines for publishing on-line, and much more.

Students are expected to . . .
- design and publish documents by using publishing software and graphic programs.

USING THE WRITING PROCESS

Overview: Our purpose in this section is to impress upon students that writing is a process of exploring and shaping meaning, not just an end product. The steps discussed in this section address different aspects of this process. "Prewriting" provides strategies for collecting possible writing ideas, experimenting with them, and eventually focusing on one for writing. "Drafting" offers suggestions for developing an idea. "Revising" helps students rethink, rework, and refine their initial writings. "Group Advising" includes guidelines and strategies for peer-review sessions. "Editing and Proofreading" offers assistance when students are ready to fine-tune a piece of writing.

A Guide to
PREWRITING

(See *Writers INC Handbook* pages 41-52.)

Major Concepts

- **Prewriting involves selecting and developing a subject.** (page 42)
- **Strategies such as journal writing, listing, freewriting, and clustering help students identify specific writing subjects.** (pages 43-45)
- **Collecting strategies, including graphic organizers, help students gather details for writing.** (pages 46-49)
- **After gathering information, a student must develop a specific focus for a subject.** (pages 50-52)

Prewriting refers to the beginning of a writing project and includes choosing a subject, gathering details about it, and organizing the details for writing. This chapter offers a variety of selecting and collecting strategies, easy-to-use graphic organizers, guidelines for forming thesis statements, and methods for organizing details. This information will be a valuable resource whenever students begin writing projects.

Students are expected to . . .
- use prewriting strategies, such as freewriting and clustering, to generate and collect ideas for writing.
- use appropriate reference materials and resources during the writing process.
- consider purpose and audience when developing writing.
- establish a central idea (focus or thesis statement), collect details, and organize supporting information for writing.

A Guide to
DRAFTING

(See *Writers INC Handbook* pages 53-58.)

Major Concepts

- **Drafting is the process of connecting the ideas the writer has collected during prewriting.** (pages 53-54)
- **A draft should be freely written, without worry about neatness or correctness.** (pages 53-54)
- **The beginning in a piece of writing should introduce the subject and interest readers; the middle should explain and/or support that subject; and the ending should bring the writing to a satisfying close.** (pages 55-58)

This chapter explains how to approach the second step in the writing process: developing the first draft. It provides guidelines and examples to help students organize the beginning, middle, and ending of their drafts.

Students are expected to . . .
- connect their thoughts after collecting details.
- apply different methods of support, including paraphrases, quotations, anecdotes, descriptions, sensory details, etc.

A Guide to
REVISING

(See *Writers INC Handbook* pages 59-68.)

Major Concepts

- **Revising deals with making changes in the writing until it says what the writer wants it to say.** (page 59)
- **Using basic revising guidelines helps students make the best revising moves.** (page 61)
- **Writers can remove uninspired ideas during later stages of revising.** (page 62)
- **Students who understand the significance of ideas, organization, and voice in writing are more likely to know what to change to improve their writing.** (pages 63-68)

This chapter presents revising as the process of improving the thoughts and details that carry the message in a piece of writing.

Students are expected to . . .
- revise drafts by adding, deleting, and rearranging copy, striving for effective content, logical organization, and appropriate voice.

A Guide to
GROUP ADVISING

(See *Writers INC Handbook* pages 69-74.)

Major Concepts

- **Understanding the roles of both writer-reader and listener-responder will help students in group-advising sessions.** (page 70)
- **Specific comments and questions give writers useful feedback for revising.** (pages 70-71)
- **Critiquing a paper, reacting to writing, appreciating good writing, and feeling your OAQS (observe-appreciate-question-suggest) are four strategies students can use in group-advising sessions.** (pages 72-73)

This chapter presents group advising as a critical component of the revising process. The text includes specific guidelines for students in their roles as writer-reader and listener-responder. In addition, it offers strategies to help students respond to their peers' writing.

Students are expected to . . .
- respond in constructive ways to others' writing.

A Guide to
EDITING and PROOFREADING

(See *Writers INC Handbook* pages 75-79.)

Major Concepts

- **Editing and proofreading involve three important traits of effective writing: sentence smoothness, word choice, and correct, accurate copy.** (page 76)
- **When editing for sentence style, writers must check for sentence problems, sentence smoothness, and sentence variety.** (page 77)
- **When editing for word choice, writers must check for common problems such as redundancy, general nouns and verbs, and the appropriateness of the level of language.** (page 78)

During the fourth step in the writing process, editing and proofreading, students prepare their writing for publication. This chapter helps students focus on effective sentence style and using the best words. Many specific problems with word choice are identified along with tactics for solving them.

Students are expected to . . .
- edit drafts to ensure effective sentence style and word choice, as well as clear, accurate copy.
- produce legible work that shows accurate spelling and correct use of punctuation and capitalization.

BASIC ELEMENTS OF WRITING

Overview: We developed "Basic Elements of Writing" with one idea in mind—to help students establish a solid foundation in the building blocks of writing. The information in "Writing Sentences" will help students express themselves clearly and correctly. The guidelines and examples in "Writing Paragraphs," "Writing Expository Essays," and "Writing Persuasive Essays" will help students write in their English classes and across the curriculum.

Writing
SENTENCES

(See *Writers INC Handbook* pages 81-94.)

Major Concepts

- **Simple sentences in English follow five basic patterns.** (page 82)
- **The most common sentence errors are fragments, comma splices, run-on sentences, and rambling sentences.** (pages 83-84)
- **Confusion in sentences can be caused by incomplete comparisons, ambiguous wording, pronoun reference problems, and misplaced and dangling modifiers.** (pages 85-86)
- **Sentences that sound artificial may contain deadwood, flowery language, etc.** (pages 87-88)
- **Sentences containing nonstandard language, double negatives, and shifts in construction are not appropriate in academic writing.** (pages 89-90)
- **There are numerous ways to combine sentences.** (page 91)
- **Modeling sentences helps students fine-tune their sense of style.** (page 92)
- **Expanding sentences can help students write more naturally and gracefully.** (page 93)

The first part of this chapter serves as a guide to sentence correctness. Students should refer to this part when they are checking their writing for sentence errors. The second part provides techniques to help students write smoother, more detailed sentences.

The list of sentence errors in this chapter is extensive. To what extent you address these errors depends on the needs of your students and the nature of your classroom.

Students are expected to . . .
- understand sentence construction (parallel structure, subordination, etc.) and proper English usage.
- edit drafts to ensure smooth-reading sentences.
- use published examples as models for writing.

Writing
PARAGRAPHS

(See *Writers INC Handbook* pages 95-104.)

Major Concepts

- **There are three parts to a paragraph: the topic sentence, the body, and the closing.** (page 96)
- **There are four basic types of paragraphs: expository, descriptive, narrative, and persuasive.** (pages 97-98)
- **Paragraph unity and details help deliver a clear message.** (page 99)
- **The details in a paragraph can be organized in seven basic ways.** (pages 100-103)

This chapter covers paragraphs as important building blocks for other kinds of writing. The basic parts and types of paragraphs are covered as are the basic methods of organization. In introductory courses, this chapter should be covered very carefully. In more advanced courses, it should be used for review and reference.

Students are expected to . . .
- establish a central idea (focus or topic sentence), collect details, and organize supporting information for writing.
- apply different methods of support, including paraphrases, quotations, anecdotes, descriptions, sensory details, etc.

Writing
EXPOSITORY Essays

(See *Writers INC Handbook* pages 105-114.)

Major Concepts

- **Writing an expository essay involves organizing specific details into an opening paragraph, several supporting paragraphs, and a closing paragraph.** (page 106)
- **To effectively develop an essay, students must adequately support a thesis.** (page 107)
- **A topic or sentence outline can be used to organize the supporting information in an essay.** (page 108)
- **Writing an expository essay is a step-by-step process.** (pages 109-113)

This chapter discusses the importance of structure, organization, and support in writing an expository essay. Once students understand the basics, they will be ready to tackle more advanced academic essays (pages 199-213). This chapter serves as an effective review for students preparing for writing-assessment tests.

> Students are expected to . . .
> - establish a central idea (focus or thesis statement), collect details, and organize supporting information for writing.
> - consider purpose and audience when developing writing.
> - prioritize information and ideas
> - conclude with a summary linked to the purpose of the composition.

Writing
PERSUASIVE Essays

(See *Writers INC Handbook* pages 115-123.)

Major Concepts

- **A persuasive essay states and supports a reasonable opinion.** (pages 115-117)
- **Writing an effective persuasive essay requires much planning, drafting, and revising.** (pages 116-117)
- **Thinking through an argument entails stating an opinion, using qualifiers, adding support, and possibly making concessions.** (pages 118-119)

- **A helpful graphic organizer, a sample essay, and an assessment rubric instruct students in writing persuasively.** (pages 120-122)

In this chapter, students are presented with the challenging task of writing essays designed to persuade. Persuasive essays require students to form and express reasonable opinions, to support their opinions with evidence, and to anticipate and address conflicting opinions.

> Students are expected to . . .
> - establish a focus or thesis statement, collect details, and organize supporting information for writing.
> - consider purpose and audience when developing their writing.
> - structure an argument in a sustained and logical fashion.
> - support a position with organized, relevant evidence.
> - anticipate and address reader concerns and counterarguments.
> - use appropriate reference resources.

THE ART OF WRITING

Overview: The chapter "Writing with Style" helps students make the best stylistic choices when they write. "Writer's Resource" identifies many techniques students may want to use in their own writing.

Writing with STYLE

(See *Writers INC Handbook* pages 125-132.)

Major Concepts

- **There are three simple rules of style: Be purposeful. Be clear. Be sincere.** (page 126)
- **Anecdotes, metaphors, and the use of repetition can add style to writing.** (pages 127-129)
- **Specific nouns, vivid verbs, and effective modifiers add style to writing.** (pages 130-131)
- **Avoid choppy sentences, passive voice, and the overuse of qualifiers in writing.** (page 132)

Impress upon students that stylistic writing begins and ends with commitment. Students must feel strongly about their writing in order to give it the proper care and attention. Make sure students know the common ailments of style and check for these problems whenever they revise and edit their work. When time permits, review the various stylistic techniques discussed in this chapter: using anecdotes, metaphors, repetition, and strong, colorful words.

> Students are expected to . . .
> • use precise language, action verbs, sensory details, appropriate modifiers, and active rather than passive voice.

Writer's RESOURCE

(See *Writers INC Handbook* pages 133-141.)

Major Concepts

- **Writing is really thinking on paper.** (page 134)
- **Writing techniques are methods used to achieve particular effects in writing.** (pages 136-138)
- **Writing terms are words used to discuss the writing process.** (pages 139-140)

This chapter contains a wide variety of valuable writing information. It charts a writer's basic thinking moves and lists possible writing topics. There are definitions and models of several dozen key writing techniques, from *allusion* to *understatement*. A glossary covers writing terms from *argumentation* to *vivid details,* and a survey of writing forms classifies writing from personal forms (like reminiscences) to business forms (like memos).

As students become familiar with this chapter, they will turn to it time and time again when they have writing-related questions.

> Students are expected to . . .
> • use appropriate reference materials and resources as needed during the writing process.

The Forms of Writing

THE FORMS OF WRITING

Overview: The first five forms of writing in this section are arranged by the type of thinking and gathering that is required of the student. For example, *personal writing* requires remembering and sharing, *subject writing* requires searching and reporting, *creative writing* requires inventing or imitating, and so on. This arrangement, based on James Moffett's "Universe of Discourse," helps students understand the different ways they can approach writing, moving from personal to public forms and from simple to complex structures. The last three forms of writing address responses to literature, research writing (MLA and APA), and business writing.

PERSONAL Writing

(See *Writers INC Handbook* pages 143-154.)

Major Concepts

- **For journal writing, students should write about things important to them and keep a writing routine.** (pages 144-146)
- **In a personal narrative, students re-create a memorable experience.** (pages 147-151)
- **In a personal essay, students share an experience and reflect upon its importance.** (pages 152-153)

This chapter focuses on three forms of personal writing: journals, personal narratives, and personal essays. Make sure that students understand these different ways that they can write about their experiences.

> Students are expected to . . .
> • write to express, discover, record, develop, and reflect on ideas.
> • create an engaging story line by employing dialogue, sensory details, specific action, and personal feelings.
> • revise and edit their writing for completeness, personal voice, specific word choice, and effective sentence style.

SUBJECT Writing

(See *Writers INC Handbook* pages 155-166.)

Major Concepts

- **Descriptive writing entails the use of vivid sensory and memory details.** (pages 156-157)
- **An eyewitness account can be developed in a number of ways and contains a wide range of sights, sounds, and smells.** (pages 158-159)
- **Successful interviews require careful planning, attentive listening, and note taking. Collected information can then be shaped into a meaningful report.** (pages 160-162)
- **To develop an effective profile, a great deal of information about the subject must be gathered through interviewing, corresponding, reading, observing, and reflecting.** (pages 163-165)

"Subject Writing" is writing to investigate and share information. This chapter may present a new cast of writing forms for students: eyewitness accounts, interview reports, profiles of a person. Explain or discuss these forms as necessary.

If you're a journalism teacher or newspaper advisor, this chapter contains forms found in most newspapers and magazines.

> Students are expected to . . .
> - use prewriting strategies to generate and organize ideas.
> - support a central idea (focus) with background information, sensory and memory details, and the subject's personal thoughts and feelings.
> - develop three key elements: characterization, setting, and action.
> - revise and edit, striving for clear, accurate, and verifiable information.

CREATIVE Writing

(See *Writers INC Handbook* pages 167-184.)

Major Concepts

- **To write a story, students must develop characters, a setting, a plot, and a theme.** (pages 168-173)
- **In a play, characters in conflict do most of the work, and they develop as the script progresses.** (pages 174-177)
- **A brief poem can capture the essence of its subject with carefully chosen words.** (pages 179-183)

The first page in this chapter establishes a point of departure for creative writing—it is the process of inventing, the process of making up something new and different. But it also has solid roots in the writer's real-world experiences and memories. Students need to know that the creative process often begins as they start exploring their own thoughts and experiences.

Basic guidelines and samples are provided for each type of writing covered in this chapter (poetry, short stories, and play scripts).

> Students are expected to . . .
> - use prewriting strategies to generate and organize ideas.
> - use sensory details and effective word choice to develop characterization, setting, and action.
> - describe and express the importance of a subject.
> - display an understanding of poetry techniques and a creative use of language.

PERSUASIVE Writing

(See *Writers INC Handbook* pages 185-198.)

Major Concepts

- **In a pet peeve essay, a student reacts to an everyday annoyance.** (pages 186-187)
- **An effective editorial presents an informed argument and a possible solution to a problem.** (pages 188-189)
- **A personal commentary can be either serious or playful while making a reflective statement about life.** (pages 190-191)
- **An essay of opposing ideas presents two or more points of view on an issue that is important to the student writer.** (pages 192-194)
- **In an essay of argumentation, a student's strong, genuine feelings about an important subject are expressed.** (pages 195-197)

Writing persuasive essays helps students learn how to form sound opinions based on facts and evidence. The writer selects a timely and debatable issue, forms and expresses a reasonable opinion about it, supports the opinion with evidence, and anticipates conflicting opinions. This chapter provides guidelines and samples for five types of persuasive writing: a pet peeve essay, an editorial, a personal commentary, an essay of opposing ideas, and an essay of argumentation.

> Students are expected to . . .
> • consider purpose and audience when developing writing.
> • structure an argument in a sustained and logical fashion.
> • support a position with organized, relevant evidence.
> • anticipate and address reader concerns and counterarguments.
> • use appropriate reference materials and resources during the writing process.

ACADEMIC Writing

(See *Writers INC Handbook* pages 199-213.)

Major Concepts
- **In a process essay, a student clearly and completely explains how something works or how to do or make something.** (pages 200-201)
- **An essay of comparison examines the similarities and differences between two or more subjects.** (pages 202-204)
- **A cause/effect essay is a thoughtful analysis of a timely subject, with clear cause/effect connections between important points related to the subject.** (pages 205-207)
- **An essay of definition thoroughly explains a term or concept.** (pages 208-209)
- **An effective problem/solution essay clearly states a problem and fully discusses possible solutions.** (pages 210-212)

In academic writing, students organize and present factual information in ways that demonstrate a clear understanding of the writing subject. This chapter includes guidelines and samples for a process essay, an essay of comparison, a cause/effect essay, an essay of definition, and a problem/solution essay.

> Students are expected to . . .
> • create compositions that state a clear purpose.
> • prioritize information from primary and secondary sources.
> • use appropriate reference materials and resources during the writing process to support the main ideas with facts, details, explanations, and examples.
> • use organizational patterns appropriate to the type of composition.
> • conclude with a summary linked to the composition's purpose.

WRITING ABOUT LITERATURE

Overview: While developing this section, the following point was foremost in our minds: Literature instruction, more than anything else, should be a special opportunity to help students find personal meaning in their reading. To meet this end, we provide students with three different ways to react to literature: forming personal responses (from journal responses to letters to an author), writing book reviews (suitable for school publications), and developing literary analyses (displaying a careful understanding of a work). Guidelines and models are provided for each type of writing. This section also includes glossaries of literary and poetry terms.

Personal
RESPONSES TO LITERATURE

(See *Writers INC Handbook* pages 215-220.)

Major Concepts
- **Personal responses to literature can include writing in a journal, writing a poem, writing a letter to the author, or developing a dialogue between the student and a specific character.** (pages 216-219)

This chapter offers samples of three types of responses to literature: letters to an author, dialogue with a character, and personal journal entries. Also included are general writing guidelines plus a set of reader-response questions for journal writing. To introduce students to the concept of responding to literature, read and discuss the opening page of this chapter. During your discussion, offer students the following quotation by Thomas Carlyle: "The best effect of any book is that it excites the reader to self-activity."

> Students are expected to . . .
> - respond to literature in a way that displays a personal connection with it.
> - develop interpretations that exhibit careful reading and understanding of significant ideas in a literary work.

Writing a
BOOK REVIEW

(See *Writers INC Handbook* pages 221-226.)

Major Concepts

- **A book review is an essay expressing a student writer's personal opinion about a book.** (pages 222-224)
- **Short reviews of books, movies, videos, and CD's are often seen in student newspapers, literary magazines, and on the Internet.** (page 225)

Writing a book review demands effective critical and evaluative skills. A successful review is informative and enjoyable to read. It highlights key parts of a book without giving the whole story away. This chapter provides guidelines for writing book reviews; sample reviews of fiction and nonfiction; and mini-reviews of other media.

> Students are expected to . . .
> - develop interpretations that exhibit careful reading and understanding of a literary work.
> - take a point of view and support it with references from the literature.

Writing a
LITERARY ANALYSIS

(See *Writers INC Handbook* pages 227-243.)

Major Concepts

- **A literary analysis presents a thoughtful examination of a literary work.** (pages 228-230)
- **Literary terms describe the different types and elements of literature.** (pages 233-241)
- **Understanding poetry and literary terms helps students discuss and write about literary works.** (pages 242-243)

An analysis is clearly the most challenging form of writing about literature. After discussing the opening page with your students, turn to the ideas for analyses listed on page 231 of the chapter. Once students see these possible starting points, the whole idea of analyzing literature will make better sense to them. You may also want to demonstrate how you would go about planning and organizing an analysis around one of these ideas. Also carefully review one of the samples, pointing out how the writing is organized and developed. When the students are ready to develop analyses of their own, discuss the general guidelines and the writing tips included in the chapter.

> Students are expected to . . .
> - develop interpretations that exhibit a careful reading and understanding of literary works.
> - demonstrate awareness of the use of stylistic devices in literature.
> - support important ideas through accurate and detailed references to the text.
> - identify and assess the impact of perceived ambiguities, nuances, and complexities within the text.

RESEARCH WRITING

Overview: "Research writing is one of the most complex intellectual activities we ask students to undertake. We are, in effect, asking them to perform the tasks of a scholar enroute to publication." This quotation comes from the Wisconsin Department of Public Instruction in their guide to curriculum planning for English. We, too, believe that writing a research paper is complex and challenging, even for the most committed and advanced high school students. For this reason, we address the different aspects of the research process in clear, easy-to-follow chapters. Emphasis is placed on responsible paraphrasing and acknowledgement of quoted sources. Both the MLA and APA styles are presented, as well as a complete MLA research paper. A Web site is available for checking citations for electronic sources.

Writing the
RESEARCH PAPER

(See *Writers INC Handbook* pages 245-254.)

Major Concepts

- **A research paper is a carefully planned essay.** (pages 245-254)
- **A research paper should be a personal process of discovery.** (page 246)

Research and report writing are important academic skills required in school and in the workplace. Research writing involves students in higher-level thinking skills (analyzing, synthesizing, and evaluating). This chapter is packed with information students need to write successful research papers. A personalized approach to research is outlined, and thorough, step-by-step guidelines are provided.

Students are expected to . . .
- select relevant topics narrow enough to be thoroughly covered.
- support the thesis with facts, details, explanations, and examples from multiple authoritative sources.
- convey information from primary and secondary sources, including technical terms, accurately.
- anticipate and address readers' potential biases and misunderstandings.
- include clear and accurate documentation.

Writing
RESPONSIBLY

(See *Writers INC Handbook* pages 255-258.)

Major Concepts

- **Writers avoid plagiarism by giving credit for anyone else's ideas or words.** (page 256)
- **In paraphrasing, writers use their own words to restate someone else's ideas; the source must be cited.** (pages 256-257)
- **Quoting material is another way to share information from another source.** (page 258)

The first part of this chapter addresses the writer's responsibility to present his or her research sincerely and honestly. During your discussion of this chapter, have students react to the following idea: *Plagiarism is really a form of intellectual thievery carried out, intentionally or unintentionally, by researchers who fail to do their own mind work.* Make sure as well that students understand what is meant by "common knowledge."

Also included in "Writing Responsibly" are guidelines for paraphrasing information from other sources and for presenting quoted materials in a research paper. Review these guidelines as needed with your students.

Students are expected to . . .
- support the thesis with facts, details, explanations, and examples from multiple authoritative sources.
- provide clear and accurate documentation in a works-cited page with their reports.

MLA Documentation Style, Sample MLA Research Paper, and APA Documentation Style

(See *Writers INC Handbook* pages 259-295.)

Major Concepts

- **In MLA and APA styles, students include parenthetical references in the body of the research paper.** (pages 260-263 and 287-288)
- **Sample works-cited entries (or references) help students document their own research.** (MLA, pages 265-274, and APA, pages 290-295)
- **Students benefit from studying a sample research paper for content and for format.** (pages 275-284)

The MLA (Modern Language Association) style manual is a popular manual in high school and college writing courses. The documentation style of the APA (American Psychological Association) is often used for papers in social science and social studies. Formatting a research paper can be done using either the MLA or APA styles. These chapters include information on citing specific sources and a sample MLA research paper.

> Students are expected to . . .
> - provide clear, accurate documentation both within their reports and in works-cited (reference) pages.

WORKPLACE WRITING

Overview: This section addresses the traditional forms of business writing—from a business letter to a memo, from an e-mail message to a proposal. Mastering the forms in this section will help students "get a job and do their job." Workplace writing will also help them right now in the school setting as they plan projects, request help, and gather materials for projects.

Writing BUSINESS LETTERS

(See *Writers INC Handbook* pages 297-308.)

Major Concepts

- **Students need to know the six parts of a business letter.** (pages 298-299)
- **There are many reasons to write business letters.** (pages 300-306)
- **There are two acceptable forms for addressing an envelope.** (page 307)

Writing good business letters can help students succeed now in school and later in the workplace. Letter writing gives students an opportunity to connect with experts and organizations that offer information, provide internships, help solve problems, and more. This chapter covers the parts of a business letter, writing guidelines, six types of business letters, and addressing envelopes.

> Students are expected to . . .
> - use the writing process to produce and send a letter.
> - follow conventional page formats, fonts, and spacing to produce an effective, readable document.
> - select a style and voice to fit the audience and purpose.
> - edit for standard usage, grammar, and mechanics.

Special Forms of
WORKPLACE
Writing

(See *Writers INC Handbook* pages 309-321.)

Major Concepts

- **Memos and e-mail messages are brief forms of writing with various functions.** (pages 310-313)
- **Effective instructions help someone complete a particular task.** (pages 314-315)
- **An attractive and informative brochure promotes a product or a cause.** (pages 316-317)
- **A proposal is a detailed plan that explains a project or fixes a problem.** (pages 318-319)
- **A résumé presents an individual to a prospective employer.** (pages 320-321)

At least 90 percent of your students will become professional writers. How so? They will earn their living, in part, by writing: memos, e-mail messages, proposals, reports, and instructions. This chapter includes the types of workplace writing students will do now and in the future. Writing guidelines and a sample are included for each form of writing.

Students are expected to . . .
- choose appropriate forms for their writing (memos, e-mail, etc.).
- select a style and voice to fit the audience and purpose.
- anticipate any reader problems or possible misunderstandings.
- use technology to produce and publish writing.

The **Tools** of Learning

SEARCHING FOR INFORMATION
Overview: The chapters in this section will help students learn how to access different types of information, gain research skills, and appreciate the importance of evaluating information before using it. Special attention is given to electronic sources of information.

Types of
INFORMATION

(See *Writers INC Handbook* pages 323-330.)

Major Concepts

- **Information sources can be divided into two categories—primary and secondary.** (page 324)
- **There are several ways to evaluate information for quality.** (page 325)
- **Information varies in how it may be "packaged"; information is located at various sites.** (pages 326-327)
- **Surveys and interviews are methods of obtaining information from primary sources.** (pages 328-330)

This chapter serves as an information guide for student researchers. The text discusses the differences between primary and secondary sources of information. It also provides a series of questions that can be used to evaluate the reliability of various resources as well as an overview of the different types of information available to students. The final part of the chapter includes guidelines for conducting surveys and interviews.

Students are expected to . . .
- use a variety of sources.
- use print and electronic indexes to locate books and articles.
- evaluate information critically and frame new questions for further investigation.

Using the
INTERNET

(See *Writers INC Handbook* pages 331-336.)

Major Concepts

- **To use the Internet effectively, students must learn how to access, evaluate, and save information.** (pages 332-334)
- **A community of writers can converse via chat rooms, mailing lists, newsgroups, and on-line writing labs on the Internet.** (page 335)
- **Net users follow Netiquette rules to communicate effectively on-line.** (page 336)

The Internet has become one of the most important research tools for students. This chapter serves as a basic guide to using the Internet as a research tool and to becoming part of the on-line community. Included are tips for locating, evaluating, and saving information found on the Net, as well as a section titled "Netiquette." (Students should be made aware of potential problems associated with Internet use—loss of privacy, quality of the information, etc.)

Students are expected to . . .
- access electronic information efficiently.
- evaluate the reliability of electronically accessed information.

Using the
LIBRARY

(See *Writers INC Handbook* pages 337-349.)

Major Concepts

- **Computer and card catalogs help students find information in libraries.** (pages 338-340)
- **Call numbers classify books (usually by the Dewey decimal system) and indicate where to find them in the library.** (pages 341-342)
- **The reference section in a library contains dictionaries, encyclopedias, thesauruses, almanacs, atlases, and more.** (page 343)
- **Knowing the parts of a book can help students find information quickly and easily.** (page 349)

Libraries are information centers that provide a variety of research services. Students will find collecting information in a library easier once they understand how the various resources are stored and accessed. This chapter covers basic library skills, including how to use a computer or card catalog, read call numbers, explore the reference section, and more.

Students are expected to . . .
- use reference materials (such as the dictionary, encyclopedia, almanac, atlas, and thesaurus) as an aid to writing.
- understand and use tables of contents, chapter and section headings, glossaries, indexes, and appendices to locate information in reference books.
- use print and electronic indexes to locate books and articles.
- access information efficiently.

READING SKILLS

Overview: *Writers INC* is first and foremost a writing handbook, but it is also a learning guide. This section of the handbook was specifically designed to help students become more productive and resourceful readers.

Research supports the fact that when students read to learn, they engage in a series of complex thought processes. In each sentence, paragraph, chart, or graph students read, they must solve certain problems before arriving at the author's meaning. The chapters in this section will help students meet their reading challenges, improve their vocabularies, and become more sophisticated readers.

Reading
GRAPHICS

(See *Writers INC Handbook* pages 351-356.)

Major Concepts

- **Graphs show how different pieces of information are related.** (pages 352-353)

- **Tables organize detailed information into rows and columns.** (page 354)
- **Picture or line diagrams are drawings designed to show how something works or how its parts relate to one another.** (page 355)
- **Maps show geographic areas for various purposes (political, road, weather, etc.).** (page 356)

Students need to understand the principles governing the interpretation of graphs, tables, diagrams, and maps. This chapter provides examples of each of these graphics, accompanied by explanations or guides to reading them.

> Students are expected to . . .
> - analyze the structure and format of graphics, and understand how authors use them to impart information.

STUDY-READING
Skills

(See *Writers INC Handbook* pages 357-366.)

Major Concepts

- **Guidelines for study-reading help students comprehend informational texts.** (page 358)
- **Knowledge of common patterns of nonfiction—description, chronological order, comparison/contrast, main idea/supporting details, cause and effect—helps students understand their reading and take notes.** (pages 359-363)
- **SQ3R is an effective strategy for reading nonfiction.** (page 364)
- **To appreciate fiction and poetry, students must read carefully and systematically.** (pages 365-366)

With each passing year, students encounter reading material that becomes more and more complex. To maintain a high level of reading comprehension, students must become more sophisticated readers. This chapter offers a broad range of strategies that will help students understand and learn from different kinds of texts. Of special interest will be the five patterns of nonfiction that students will often encounter in their nonfiction reading. For each

pattern there is a brief explanation, a sample text, and a graphic organizer that students can use when taking notes.

> Students are expected to . . .
> - take efficient notes from sources such as periodicals and books.
> - evaluate the credibility of an author's argument or position.

Improving
VOCABULARY
Skills

(See *Writers INC Handbook* pages 367-381.)

Major Concepts

- **Students may increase their vocabularies by keeping vocabulary notebooks, making flash cards, using thesauruses, and more.** (page 368)
- **Context helps students figure out unfamiliar words.** (pages 369-370)
- **When students know the meanings of prefixes, suffixes, and word roots, they can figure out the meanings of words that contain those parts.** (pages 371-381)

When students know how to improve their word knowledge, they become more confident and independent readers. This chapter offers eight strategies for building vocabularies. It also lists six common types of context clues and provides a comprehensive glossary of common prefixes, suffixes, and roots.

> Students are expected to . . .
> - learn vocabulary-building strategies.
> - know and use common prefixes, suffixes, and roots.

STUDY SKILLS

Overview: This section contains chapters on classroom skills (group skills, planning skills, etc.), listening and note taking, writing to learn, and test taking. All of this information is designed to help students become better learners and to improve their performance across the curriculum. A special feature of the test-taking chapter is the information on taking district or state writing tests.

Improving
CLASSROOM Skills

(See *Writers INC Handbook* pages 383-388.)

Major Concepts

- **Key group skills are listening, observing, cooperating, clarifying, and responding.** (pages 384-386)
- **Time-management skills help students learn to use their time wisely.** (page 387)
- **Completing assignments is easier when students plan ahead.** (page 388)

To do well in school, students must possess the planning and group skills covered in this chapter. As you discuss the strategies, guidelines, or ideas presented in "Classroom Skills," link the information to your students' needs. Also consider bringing in an expert to talk about how important these skills are—both in school and in the workplace.

Students are expected to . . .
- form judgments about ideas under discussion and support those judgments with sound evidence.
- effectively participate and contribute to group projects.
- become independent and confident learners.

LISTENING and
NOTE-TAKING Skills

(See *Writers INC Handbook* pages 389-396.)

Major Concepts

- **To listen well, students must concentrate on what is being said.** (pages 390-391)
- **Note taking involves listening, thinking, reacting, questioning, summarizing, organizing, labeling, and writing.** (pages 392-393)
- **Note-taking guides help students take textbook, lecture, and review notes.** (pages 394-395)
- **A personal shorthand system makes note taking easier.** (page 396)

Taking good notes requires the effort of listening well. In fact, listening and note taking work hand in hand. Ten ways to improve listening skills are explained in this chapter. In addition, there are guidelines and strategies to help students develop good note-taking skills, as well as sample note-taking guides.

Students are expected to . . .
- take notes from sources such as guest speakers, periodicals, books, on-line sites, and so on.
- summarize and organize ideas gained from multiple sources.

Writing to
LEARN

(See *Writers INC Handbook* pages 397-404.)

Major Concepts

- **Learning logs allow students to explore important ideas and concepts they are studying.** (pages 398-399)
- **A paraphrase is a type of summary that may include a student's interpretation of a passage.** (page 402)
- **Writing a summary helps students understand and remember what they have read.** (pages 403-404)

This chapter explores writing as a learning tool. The text introduces students to learning logs and other writing-to-learn activities. It also provides guidelines for writing paraphrases and summaries. When discussing this chapter, encourage students to keep a learning log. Also have students experiment with various writing-to-learn activities throughout the school year.

> Students are expected to . . .
> • use writing as a learning tool.
> • write summaries that contain the material's main ideas and most significant details.

TEST-TAKING
Skills

(See *Writers INC Handbook* pages 405-419.)

Major Concepts

- **Taking an essay test involves understanding each question's key words and then planning and writing thoughtful answers.** (pages 406-409)
- **Guidelines for taking an objective test (true/false, matching, multiple choice) help students avoid common pitfalls.** (page 411)
- **When students are familiar with the format that standardized tests follow, they are better prepared to take the tests.** (pages 413-414)
- **Students can become more skilled at planning and writing impromptu essays.** (pages 415-419)

This chapter provides a number of guidelines, strategies, and samples to help students improve their test-taking performance. Guide students through the information in this chapter so that they may be better prepared for all test situations—including essay tests, objective tests, standardized tests, and timed writing tests. You may even want to take students through one or two trial tests to make sure they understand all of the steps in the process.

> Students are expected to . . .
> • demonstrate comprehensive understanding of important ideas.
> • integrate specific information and make broader applications or generalizations.

SPEAKING, THINKING, AND VIEWING SKILLS

Overview: Most experts in the field of communication would agree that there are five basic communication functions: expressing feelings, ritualizing (greeting, taking leave, praying, etc.), imagining, informing, and persuading. The last three functions listed here should be addressed in any secondary language arts curriculum. "Speech Skills" in *Writers INC* will best serve students when they are preparing speeches to inform and persuade, the two communication functions requiring the most planning. "Multimedia Reports" shows students how to make traditional speeches more interactive and visual.

"Thinking Skills" will help students learn how to use six types of thinking in their daily schoolwork. The chapter also explores how effective explanations and arguments are built on evidence and logic.

"Viewing Skills" helps students think about and question what they see on television, videos, and Web sites. With the proper training, students can become thoughtful, objective viewers.

SPEECH Skills

(See *Writers INC Handbook* pages 421-432.)

Major Concepts

- **Planning a speech requires close attention to purpose, subject, audience, and details.** (pages 422-423)
- **An effective introduction, body, and conclusion help a student deliver an interesting speech whether using note cards, an outline, or a manuscript.** (pages 424-429)
- **Rehearsing is an important part of the speaking process.** (page 430)
- **Use of an appropriate style and tone strengthens the spoken word.** (pages 431-432)

The ability to speak clearly, confidently, and persuasively is a skill that students need to master for school and the workplace. This chapter is a step-by-step guide to preparing and giving a speech, from planning to writing to rehearsing. It also takes a close look at the style and tone of speeches. As part of your introduction to "Speech Skills," have your students react to the following quotation by Dorothy Sarnoff: "Make sure you have finished speaking before your audience has finished listening." This quotation suggests a number of important points related to the speech-making process: Speakers must have something worthwhile to say, they must get to the point, they must deliver their ideas in an interesting way, and so on.

For students to prepare effective speeches, they need more than a handbook chapter can provide. They need to observe (hear) and evaluate experienced speakers in action. There are individuals in most communities ready to contribute their time and speaking expertise if you ask them. When in-person observations are impossible, you can use videotapes or recordings of speakers.

> Students are expected to . . .
> - choose appropriate patterns of organization for speeches.
> - use various techniques to develop introductions and conclusions (quotations, stories, references to an expert source).
> - present a clear thesis and use valid, relevant supporting information.
> - analyze the audience and choose appropriate language and nonverbal techniques.

MULTIMEDIA
Reports
(See *Writers INC Handbook* pages 433-436.)

Major Concepts
- **A computer multimedia presentation adds another dimension to a speech.** (page 434)
- **An interactive report links text, images, and other information for a viewer.** (page 435)

Today's scholars—tomorrow's business people—must be able to use technology to deliver reports and presentations. Personal computers allow students to make their reports and presen-tations multisensory. Speakers can carry an entire library of visual aids on a computer. This chapter contains writing guidelines for creating a multimedia presentation and an interactive report. Samples of each are available on the Write Source Web site <thewritesource.com>.

> Students are expected to . . .
> - use available technology to shape and present an effective speech or report.
> - combine text, images, and sounds from a range of sources.

THINKING
Skills
(See *Writers INC Handbook* pages 437-446.)

Major Concepts
- **Recalling requires remembering and repeating.** (page 439)
- **Understanding information involves explaining, describing, and telling how something works.** (page 440)
- **Applying involves demonstrating, showing, or using information.** (page 441)
- **Analyzing means breaking down information into smaller parts.** (page 442)
- **Synthesizing information includes predicting, inventing, and redesigning.** (page 443)
- **Evaluating requires thorough understanding and analysis of a subject.** (page 444)
- **Students can learn to avoid logical fallacies in their writing.** (pages 445-446)

Learning different ways to think about ideas, issues, and problems helps students complete their most challenging academic tasks. This chapter explains six levels of thinking that will help students make decisions, solve problems, ask questions, think logically, and more. The chapter concludes with ways to recognize and avoid "fuzzy thinking."

To emphasize the value of thinking skills, have various good thinkers speak to your class. You could ask a local attorney to explain how he or she prepares and presents a convincing case. A physician could describe how he or she makes a diagnosis, prepares and carries out an operation, and proposes a plan for recovery. A car mechanic could explain what it means to "trou-bleshoot" and share some challenging car problems he or she has dealt with. A coach could describe how he or she prepares a game plan for an upcoming opponent, and so on.

> Students are expected to . . .
> - use different levels of thinking to complete their writing and learning tasks.
> - synthesize information from multiple sources.
> - identify faulty logic or inconsistencies in various media sources.

VIEWING Skills

(See *Writers INC Handbook* pages 447-453.)

Major Concepts

- **Students should assess television news reports for completeness, correctness, and balance.** (pages 448-449)
- **Writing about a television show or a video helps students better understand the presentation.** (pages 450-451)
- **Many commercials rely on subtle, hidden messages.** (page 452)
- **Determining the reliability of Web sites involves asking questions and watching for various "red flags."** (page 453)

Television and the World Wide Web have a huge impact on what students know and think about the world. It's important that students learn strategies to evaluate and question what they view—and have opportunities to use these strategies. This chapter helps them become critical viewers of TV news, videos, commercials, and Web sites.

> Students are expected to . . .
> - evaluate the ways in which media (TV news, on-line information, documentaries, and so on) cover different events.
> - make distinctions between the importance of various data, facts, or ideas.

Proofreader's Guide

Overview: You will note that we've placed the "Proofreader's Guide" near the end of the handbook—after all of the guidelines for writing and learning. We did this to emphasize the fact that writing and language learning shouldn't begin with the study of grammar. The conventions of language take on real meaning when students are ready to share what they have learned. Our intention here is not to downplay the importance of grammar or punctuation. Students need a working knowledge of the standard use and presentation of their language. However, we suggest that you put grammar and mechanics in proper perspective and not make them the focus of your writing program.

The "Proofreader's Guide" is divided into five main parts: "Marking Punctuation," "Checking Mechanics," "Using the Right Word," "Parts of Speech," and "Using the Language." Each one of the five parts contains explanations and examples to illustrate the basic rules. "Using the Language" deals with different aspects of sentences, diagramming sentences, and using fair language in communication.

Student Almanac

Overview: The "Student Almanac" helps make *Writers INC* a general, all-purpose reference book that students can use in all of their classes. This section includes useful tables and charts (including conversion tables), full-color world maps, and an extensive historical time line. The time line contains three different categories of historical events: "U.S. and World History," "Science & Inventions," and "Literature & Life."

To introduce students to this section, have them list their classes across the top or along the side of a piece of paper. Then have them identify the parts of the "Student Almanac" that will help them in each of their classes.

Approaches to Writing

The approaches to writing described on the following pages offer you a variety of ways to meet the individual needs of your students.

Effective Writing Instruction

Contemporary writing research shows us that writing isn't really taught. That is, writing isn't a set of facts, forms, or formulas that a teacher imparts, and it certainly isn't worksheet busywork. We know that it is (or should be) a student-centered activity that is learned through a variety of writing experiences.

The teacher's role in effective writing programs changes from lecturer to mentor as teachers and students write and learn together. By providing the proper mixture of freedom, encouragement, and guidance, writing teachers create environments that promote writing as a student-centered learning activity. Writing approaches that demonstrate this philosophy share two basic goals:

1 **Students learn to write.** Students learn to write in the same way all writers learn—by practicing the craft. The best writing programs give students frequent, significant, and varied writing opportunities. Students write for many purposes and for many audiences. They receive constructive, supportive, and challenging responses to their writing as well as timely instruction designed to meet their individual needs.

2 **Students write to learn.** Writing is thinking on paper. Through writing, students explore ideas and questions—about themselves, about the world, about subjects they're studying in school. Students in effective writing programs write to understand, discover, clarify thinking, and pass along information.

In addition, effective writing programs share the following characteristics:

No textbook needed: Most textbooks by their very nature are prescriptive. They are designed to teach writing skills, but they are also intended to tie the teacher and student to the textbook. Good writing programs encourage independent thinking and use the students' own writing as the text. Supported by the necessary reference materials (including a handbook), students and teachers help one another develop and grow as writers.

Individualized: Because all writers are unique, one formula for writing doesn't work for all students at the same time. Strong writing programs allow students to write and work individually. The teacher provides assistance and instruction as it is needed—usually in the form of a 10- to 15-minute minilesson about a basic skill or rhetorical concept.

Interactive classroom structure: Strong writing programs promote active learning. Writing classrooms are structured to reflect real writing experiences. Students interact with one another and with the teacher to discuss their writing. On a given day, a student might spend time in a group critiquing session, work on a project of his or her own, or help a classmate sort out a writing problem. There's no hiding in the last row of the classroom as the teacher lectures.

Well planned: Just because effective writing programs are student centered doesn't mean that students can simply do as they please. Even the most motivated students will take advantage of too much freedom. Deadlines, support materials, methods of instruction, methods of measuring writing progress, and sensible classroom management procedures all have to be established for a program to be successful.

Adaptable and integrated curriculum: A good writing program is flexible. It must accommodate new methods of writing instruction or assessment. If an existing method or routine doesn't work well with a particular group of students, changes are made. Likewise, a good writing program combines various approaches to provide the best writing opportunities for the students. What follows is a brief description of five significant approaches to writing.

An Overview of the Approaches

As you begin your search for an appropriate writing approach, remember that these five approaches are not exclusive. One approach can be used in conjunction with other writing approaches. When designing a writing program, choose an approach (or a combination) that fits the needs of you and your students. Remember, you must provide students with guidelines and strategies for approaching writing as well as numerous opportunities to practice what they learn.

1 The Personal-Experience Approach

The focus of this approach is simple: students enjoy writing and find it meaningful if it stems from their personal experiences and observations. Students usually keep a journal in a personal-experience (experiential) program so that they always have a number of potential writing ideas to draw from. Often the writing process and some form of writing workshop are incorporated into the program.

Freewriting (spontaneous writing) also plays a key role in this approach to writing. Both freewriting and journal writing help students write honestly about their personal experiences when they do assigned writing. And these techniques help students eventually produce writing that readers will find interesting and entertaining.

Review the forms of writing in *Writers INC* (page 141), and you will note that we generally address personal forms of writing before we address content-oriented forms of writing. The more students write from personal experience, the better able they are to address increasingly complex experiences in more sophisticated forms of writing. (See page 57 in this guide for more information.) For more about the personal-experience approach, read Ken Macrorie's *Writing to Be Read* and *The I-Search Paper* as well as James Moffet's Active Voices series.

"The interior view of the writing process makes it clear that the writing course should have one central purpose: to allow students to use language to explore [their] world."
—C. Day-Lewis

2 The Process Approach

While using the process approach, students learn that writing—real writing—is a process of exploration and discovery rather than an end product or a series of basic skills. As students develop their writing, they make use of all steps in the writing process—prewriting, drafting, revising, editing and proofreading, and publishing. And the writing they develop, for the most part, stems from their own experiences and thinking.

Students use prewriting activities to discover writing ideas they know and care about. They are encouraged to talk about their ideas and create a classroom community of writers. They write first drafts freely and quickly, and they revise carefully. After editing and proofreading, students share or publish their work.

Writers INC discusses the writing process (starting on page 3). Also note that the guidelines for the specific forms of writing are organized according to the steps in the writing process. (See pages 58-59 in this guide for more on the writing process.) For more about the writing process, read *What a Writer Needs* by Ralph Fletcher and *Teaching Grammar in Context* by Constance Weaver.

3 The Thematic Approach

When using this approach, the teacher (with student input) chooses a theme (such as change, power, courage, etc.) that serves as the focal point for an intense, integrated language experience—an experience that immerses students in integrated reading, writing, and speaking activities that may cross into other curricular areas.

The writing teacher provides pieces of literature and other prewriting activities as starting points for the thematic study. Students then explore the theme from different perspectives and eventually focus on one aspect of the theme. Writing projects evolve from these activities.

Thematic teaching isn't just for English class. Teachers of any other content area can also be thematic teachers. In addition, teams of teachers from various disciplines can work together by choosing a theme and integrating writing, reading, speaking, and listening activities in different content areas. These interdisciplinary thematic units can provide students with complete language experiences that will actively involve them in learning. (See page 60 in this guide.) For more about interdisciplinary teaching and the thematic approach, read *Restructuring for an Interdisciplinary Curriculum,* edited by John M. Jenkins and Daniel Turner (NASSP).

"[*Active Voices*] is not a particular approach based on writing 'exercises' . . . In fact, it challenges such an approach and insists that only within some whole actual discourse based on individual thinking can words, sentences, and paragraphs be meaningfully practiced and examined." —James Moffett

4 The Trait-Based Approach

Students who use a trait-based approach to writing become confident, competent managers of their own writing process. In particular, they learn how to approach revision because they know what makes writing work.

Trait-based instruction focuses on key features—or traits—that most writers, editors, and thoughtful readers agree are essential to effective writing. These traits are as follows:
- stimulating ideas
- logical organization
- personal voice
- original word choice
- effective sentence style
- correct, accurate copy

Students are taught each trait individually, but eventually they address all of them as they revise and edit their own work. The strength of trait-based instruction lies in its power to make writing and revision manageable for students.

Like an athletic coach, a trait-based writing instructor helps students develop overall proficiency one critical skill at a time. (See page 61 in this guide.) For more about the trait-based approach, read *Creating Writers* by Vicki Spandel and Richard J. Stiggins.

5 The Writing Workshop Approach

In a writing workshop, students write or work on writing-related issues every day (reading, researching, critiquing, participating in collaborative writing, etc.). They keep all of their writing in folders, and they produce a specified number of finished pieces by the end of the term. They are encouraged to take risks and to experiment with new forms and techniques. Support during each writing project comes from both peer and teacher conferences. Students use the steps in the writing process to develop their writing and share it with the group.

The teacher acts as a guide and facilitator, creating a classroom environment that is conducive to a workshop. Desks are arranged for student interaction, and the classroom is stocked with relevant reading and writing materials. Instruction and advice are given as they are needed—on an individual basis, in small groups, or to the entire class. (See page 62 in this guide.) For more about the writing workshop approach, read *Seeking Diversity* by Linda Rief, *The Art of Teaching Writing* by Lucy McCormick Calkins, *Crafting a Life in Essay, Story, Poem* by Donald M. Murray, or *The Writing Workshop, Volumes 1 & 2* by Alan Ziegler.

The Personal-Experience Approach

The focus of this approach is simple: students enjoy writing that stems from their own experiences and observations. Developing personal writing skills prepares students to address more complex content-oriented writing.

Getting Started

Before you begin to implement this approach, remember these key points:

- The personal approach incorporates the writing process and the writing workshop.
- Journals, a key component of the personal approach, can be used in many ways to accomplish different goals.
- The audience and purpose for this type of writing change as the writer moves from a personal to a more formal style of writing.

Implementation Guidelines

- Establish a classroom environment that invites students to write by providing stimulating topic ideas—through books, magazines, posters, displays, etc.
- Help students become more comfortable with writing by establishing a weekly routine for journal writing.
- Establish the purpose and audience for student writing. Will the writing be shared with the teacher? With other students?

Teaching Strategies

In addition to the strategies provided in *Writers INC*, try these ideas:

JOURNALS

Diary ℮ In this journal, students record their thoughts and feelings. Due to the private nature of this type of writing, it may or may not be shared.

Freewrite Journal ℮ This teacher-directed journal offers writing prompts that direct students to explore ideas in daily 10-minute quick writes.

Dialogue Journal ℮ The teacher and student write back and forth to one another in this type of journal. Dialogue may be personal or related to a subject area being studied.

Personal Notebook ℮ In this journal, students record ideas, observations, and insights that they may use in future writing pieces.

Class or Project Journal ℮ In this journal, students respond to what they are reading or studying in class. Questions, predictions, and commentary are common in this type of journal. For a group project, students document their participation and responsibilities, as well as evaluations of the group's performance.

Learning Log ℮ In this journal, students record what they are learning. In science, this could be an observation log for a lab experiment. In social studies, this could be a freewrite exploring the relationship between what is being studied and students' past experiences or knowledge.

RESEARCH (I-Search)

Journals ℮ After students choose a topic that interests them, allow them to explore the topic through mapping or brainstorming. Then have them write to explore different perspectives on their topic, taking notes as they conduct an interview or carry on a dialogue with an "expert." They should keep a log, recording questions that arise during the process, as well as answers and other discoveries. Students should also record their responses to and summaries of background reading on the topic.

Research Report ℮ This formal report includes personal connections students make with the topic. As they improve their research skills, their research reports become more sophisticated.

INFORMAL TO FORMAL

Transitions from personal to more complex forms could include the following:

Informal	Formal
Sensory freewriting	Observation reports
	Descriptions
Discussions of topics	Essays
Brainstorming	Speeches
Mapping	Editorials
Dialogue journals	One-act plays
Freewrite monologues	Argumentation essays
Story starters	Short stories
Dreams	Poetry
Writing prompts	Narratives

The Process Approach

This approach emphasizes the process of exploring and discovering in writing rather than the end product. In the process approach, writing is viewed as a developmental process rather than an accumulation of skills. *Writers INC* divides the process into these steps: prewriting, writing, revising, editing and proofreading, and publishing.

Getting Started

Before you begin to implement the process approach, remember these key points:

○ The writing process is not linear; it is cyclical. Steps are repeated in different order depending on the writers and the writing assignments.

○ The writing process is unique for each writer.

○ Writing is not a neat, formulaic, or orderly process.

○ Not all writing needs to progress through all the stages of the writing process.

○ Considering audience and purpose helps writers develop a piece of writing.

○ Because the writing process helps turn thinking into writing, it's valuable in all content areas.

Implementation Guidelines

○ Help students understand and model the stages of the writing process so that they can individualize the steps to meet their own writing needs.

○ Give students many opportunities to practice the steps of the writing process— especially prewriting and revising, steps that weaker writers tend to ignore.

○ Write with your students to show them that you are not just an evaluator, but also a writer.

○ Encourage students to think about their writing process and write reflectively about it as they develop a piece.

○ Emphasize creativity and exploration (rather than perfection) during prewriting and drafting; stress organization during revising; focus on refinement during editing and proofreading.

○ Use writing folders to store "in progress" work.

Teaching Strategies

In addition to the prewriting, drafting, revising, editing and proofreading, and publishing strategies offered in *Writers INC*, try these ideas:

■ PREWRITING

While prewriting strategies are designed to stimulate the flow of ideas before any structured writing begins, they can also help writers explore ideas throughout the writing process. In prewriting, the writer discovers expected and unexpected relationships between ideas and experiments with ways of developing and supporting these ideas.

Color-Coded Cluster @ Color coding can help identify related ideas during the exploration process. For example, students may explore and cluster a topic by using the five senses, coding each sense by color. Such coding can also be used to highlight ideas according to patterns of organization—cause and effect, problem and solution, pro and con, comparison and contrast.

Branching @ Organizers and graphs provide a tighter structure for the exploration process. (See pages 48-49 in *Writers INC* for more on graphic organizers.)

Musical Freewriting @ Accompany student writing with music to create a specific mood. This prewriting activity encourages students to explore a topic from different perspectives.

Question Clusters @ Have students cluster by focusing on the journalist's questions (who? what? when? where? why? and how?) to develop their ideas.

■ DRAFTING

The drafting stage should be spontaneous and creative—the process of shaping and connecting ideas. In this stage, writers learn what they have to say about a topic. This experimental, chaotic, and often messy process takes time, energy, patience, and persistence.

Great Authors, Great Ideas @ Read aloud some great leads and endings. Choose different styles so that students don't become convinced that there is only one way to write an introduction or ending. Put examples from various forms of writing on the overhead, read them, and discuss what makes these introductions and conclusions work. Then give students opportunities to experiment with different introductions and conclusions of their own.

Teacher Drafters @ Share one of your own drafts with your students. Allow them to see how messy and disorganized this stage can be for you.

For Whom Am I Writing? @ Practice writing to different audiences and for different purposes. Have students write letters or directions on the same topic to elderly relatives and friends, to students in other classes, and to younger students. Discuss how the audience affects the writing.

Sound Check @ Good writing is communication between the writer and the reader. Ask students to explain their topic to someone else by pretending to be talking to the reader. Have them focus on making their ideas understandable and interesting.

■ REVISING

Revision is the act of "looking again" at a piece of writing with an eye for improving it. Remind students that any writing they take to finished form must be thoroughly revised before it will be effective.

Teacher Revisers @ Make an overhead of one of your first drafts, and discuss its strengths and weaknesses with students. Then show them your revision work and your second draft.

Expanding and Contracting @ Ask students to expand a professional writing model by adding concrete details and specific support. Compare it to the original and discuss reasons for expanding a piece of writing. Then ask students to narrow the focus of a writing model to be more specific.

Building Strong Connections @ Take a short story with strong transitions, cut it into sections, and mix them up. Then have students reassemble the story by using the transitions to connect ideas. The story "Charles" by Shirley Jackson works well for this activity. Another idea is to cut a paragraph into sentences and have students reassemble it in outline form.

Freewriting Frenzy @ Have students choose from their own journal freewrites and experiment with writing for a different audience, changing the form or purpose, experimenting with different patterns of organization, or changing the point of view.

■ EDITING AND PROOFREADING

Editing and proofreading involve line-by-line changes that make a piece of writing readable and accurate. Editing is most effective when teachers hold regular editing conferences with students, and when students learn to approach editing as a process of fine-tuning and correcting a piece of writing after it has been revised.

Read It Out Loud @ Assign student partners to read each other's drafts out loud, or have students tape-record their own drafts. Hearing a piece of writing is an effective way to check for sentence smoothness, word choice, and accuracy.

Post It @ Make posters of some common usage problems and post them around the room.

Model Correctness @ Provide class editing and proofreading practice by correcting sample paragraphs together on an overhead.

Bloopers @ Have students target errors in newspapers, magazines, newsletters, and advertisements. Offer rewards to "typo terminators."

Focus @ Have students edit for one kind of error at a time. As they become adept at seeing errors, they may concentrate on more than one type of error at a time.

■ PUBLISHING

Publishing is the driving force behind writing. It makes all of a student's prewriting, drafting, revising, and editing worth the effort. Publishing can take many forms.

Publishing in Process @ When students read their writing to a partner, they get immediate feedback and reaction; this directs further writing. Read out loud from your own work and solicit responses from the class, using appropriate response guidelines on pages 70-73 in *Writers INC*.

Quotable Quotations @ Each week, put a passage of student writing on the board as a model of good writing. (Get permission first and allow the writer to remain anonymous.)

Literary Magazine @ Have the class publish stories, poems, and essays in a literary magazine made available to the entire student body.

Real-World Writers @ Have students write letters of inquiry and/or application to an individual outside of the school setting.

The Thematic Approach

The thematic approach to writing helps students use language meaningfully to identify relationships within and between content areas. With this approach, a teacher or team of teachers chooses a theme to serve as the focus of an integrated learning experience that combines writing, reading, speaking, and listening skills.

Getting Started

Before you begin to implement the thematic approach, remember these key points:

- The thematic approach can be used to study one discipline or it can span the disciplines.
- Thematic writing provides an avenue for students to write to learn—to connect their learning (synthesize and integrate), to apply it to new situations, and to think creatively.
- While students contribute to decisions about the type of writing project, its length, its audience, and the time schedule, teachers guide them through the writing process.

Implementation Guidelines

- Thematic projects may be written individually, in small groups, or as a class.
- This approach incorporates the process approach. Familiarize students with the steps of the writing process before you begin.
- Writing activities should reflect clear objectives and begin only after students are grounded in the content area or theme.
- A topic should be selected that is neither too general nor too specific, one that is relevant and interesting to students.
- As a framework for exploration, specific questions can provide a "table of contents," a scope and a sequence for the thematic study.
- Writing assignments in different content areas should involve inquiry, discovery, and synthesis, rather than mere recitation of factual information.

Teaching Strategies
CHOOSING A THEME OR TOPIC

Teacher-Chosen Theme @ Discuss interesting material about the theme. Then collaborate with students about how to explore the theme.

Student-Chosen Theme @ Brainstorm for interesting topics and write them on the board. In small groups, have students cluster a theme. List the topic in the center with spokes representing other subjects or areas of literacy (writing, speaking, listening, thinking, reading).

Continue Exploring @ Talk about and list various audiences and how they would affect the handling of this theme.

Resources @ Provide reading material relevant to the theme. Encourage the use of both primary and secondary research materials.

ORGANIZING THE THEMATIC STUDY

Create a Framework @ In discussion, develop questions that the thematic study will answer. Post them as reminders to students about the scope and focus of their exploration.

DURING THE THEMATIC STUDY

Other Voices @ Have students interview community members who are familiar with the theme. Invite speakers. Schedule video presentations.

Synthesize and Integrate Information @ Have students write to enlarge their perspectives. Employ whole-class and small-group activities:

- speeches
- magazines
- one-act plays
- newspapers
- presentations
- student-poetry anthologies
- debates
- multimedia

Individual writing activities:

- journals
- editorials
- cartoons
- book reviews
- research papers
- interviews
- proposals
- personal essays
- problem/solution essays
- argumentation essays
- letters of complaint
- observation reports
- song compositions

AFTER THE THEMATIC STUDY

Publish @ Create a class newspaper, anthology, magazine, research report, or multimedia presentation.

Perform @ Present plays, speeches, or debates.

Display @ Design a bulletin board or Web site.

Share @ Invite other classes, family, and friends to an open house.

The Trait-Based Approach

Trait-based writing can be integrated into the writing process and a writing workshop. This approach focuses on helping students identify, in their own writing and in the writing of others, those qualities that make writing strong.

Getting Started

Before you begin implementing the trait-based approach, remember these key points:

○ The trait-based approach helps students to become good assessors of all writing and to improve their own writing.

○ Check *Writers INC* (pages 21-26) and page 81 in this teacher's guide for more information on the traits.

Implementation Guidelines

○ Use writing models from books, newspapers, menus, travel brochures, and the workplace. Discuss how the traits of effective writing are (or are not) demonstrated in each model.

○ Use real models to teach the traits separately, taking time for students to understand each trait.

○ Display posters illustrating the traits.

○ Use trait language to respond to student writing; ask students to use trait language to respond to one another's writing.

○ Once a week, as a class, score a piece of anonymous writing to help refine students' assessment skills.

○ Hold peer-response sessions during which students can discuss their writing according to the traits.

○ Give students rubrics (scoring guides) before they begin writing, so they understand what is expected for each writing task.

Teaching Strategies

IDEAS

Textbook Ideas @ In small groups, have students find a textbook section that shows good idea development. As a class, discuss this trait.

Pick a Paragraph @ Using paragraphs from newspapers, recipes, advertisements, and so on, discuss the idea development of each sample.

ORGANIZATION

From the Pros @ Choose a professional piece of writing with excellent transitions, cut it into pieces, and have small groups reassemble it. Discuss how transitions aid organization.

From Start to Finish @ Look at introductions (and conclusions) from pieces by professional writers. Discuss what makes the introductions and conclusions "work." Have students model good introductions and conclusions for their own writing.

VOICE

Imaginary Conversations @ Have students write about a stormy night using two different voices—one calm, the other panicky. Share the freewrites and discuss how the voices affect the writing.

Audience Adjustment @ Have students write three sets of instructions for the same task: one set for a child, one for an elderly friend, and one for a classmate. How do the three voices vary?

WORD CHOICE

Workouts with Words @ Using pieces of their own writing, have students identify strong and weak word choices. Then have them revise their work by replacing general words with vivid ones.

Theme Dictionaries @ Have students create dictionaries according to their areas of interest: music, sports, technology, etc.

SENTENCE STYLE

Paragraph Makeovers @ Give students two paragraphs: one with short, choppy sentences and the other with only one long sentence. Ask them to rewrite each paragraph by changing the sentence lengths.

Test Textbooks @ Using textbooks, have students chart sentence lengths, beginnings, and transitions. Discuss the differences and similarities among the texts.

ACCURACY

Reward Offered @ Reward students for finding mechanical errors in your work.

Editor's Desk @ Have students use copy editors' symbols in their editing work.

The Writing Workshop Approach

The writing workshop approach offers students a writing experience that is similar to a real-world writing experience. In this approach, students write independently; they choose their own topics and spend the class period working through stages of the writing process that apply to their topics and writing needs. Like professional writers who get feedback on their writing from editors and publishers, student writers get support for their writing from their peers and teacher during conferences.

Getting Started

Before you begin to implement this approach, remember these key points:

○ This approach establishes a writing community as students and teacher work collaboratively through the writing process.

○ In an informal workshop classroom, the teacher serves as a writing mentor.

○ Each class period focuses on providing students with a large block of time to work on writing projects of their choice.

○ Depending on the group's needs, the teacher may use class time to discuss writing issues, address questions, and share professional models to guide the writing process.

○ Students work through the steps of the writing process at their own pace, conferring with other students and the teacher as necessary.

○ Students write daily for a set period of time.

○ Students use writing folders for both finished and unfinished pieces. For each marking period, students choose two or three pieces to develop for a grade assessment.

Implementation Guidelines

○ Despite the relaxed classroom structure of this approach, routines must be maintained. (See the class schedule in the next column.)

○ Establish areas for certain tasks: writing area, conferencing area, editing and proofreading area, publishing area.

○ Stock the classroom with interactive, stimulating resources.

○ Share examples of your own writing, including problems you've encountered as well as ways you've tried to solve those problems.

○ Establish your role as a facilitator—responding to, encouraging, and even challenging students as they develop their ideas through the writing process.

Teaching Strategies

Study the sample schedule below, showing how one teacher organized a writing workshop.

Since the schedule was designed for one of the first weeks of the workshop, all students were asked to participate in the minilessons. This plan would change, of course, according to the group's needs. One teacher might conduct writing workshops for three days a week and reading workshops for the other two days. Another teacher might vary the routine to conduct an extended lesson dealing with an important writing skill. Another teacher might conduct minilessons two or three days a week and have students write in a journal on the other days.

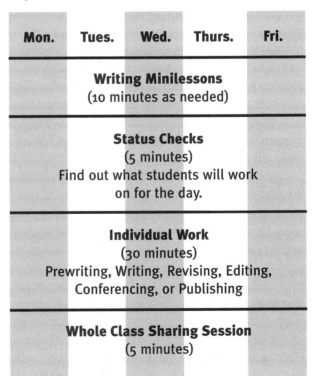

Mon.	Tues.	Wed.	Thurs.	Fri.
Writing Minilessons (10 minutes as needed)				
Status Checks (5 minutes) Find out what students will work on for the day.				
Individual Work (30 minutes) Prewriting, Writing, Revising, Editing, Conferencing, or Publishing				
Whole Class Sharing Session (5 minutes)				

Schoolwide Writing

The strategies and guidelines discussed in this chapter will help you make writing an important part of your curriculum whether you teach mathematics, science, social studies, or English.

Introduction to Writing Across the Curriculum

"I hear and I forget;
I see and I remember;
I write and I understand."

—Chinese proverb

Q. What is writing across the curriculum?

A. Writing across the curriculum (WAC) is the use of writing as a teaching and learning tool in all courses. Based on his or her course content and learning goals, each teacher chooses which writing activities to use and how to use them.

Q. Why should students write in all courses?

A. Cross-curricular writing activities help students in three ways:

1. to think through and find meaning in their learning,
2. to retain what they learn, and
3. to develop their writing skills.

In his book *Smart Schools,* David Perkins argues that writing presses students to think. In turn, that thinking helps students construct a network of meaning that connects lessons within a course, courses within a curriculum, and a curriculum to students' plans for the future. When students find meaning in their learning, they have the incentive to work hard and to retain what they learn.

In their book *Writing to Learn / Learning to Write,* authors Mayher, Lester, and Pradl also argue that writing helps students learn. But WAC, say the authors, has an additional benefit: while students are writing to learn, they're also learning to write. WAC activities give students practice in writing skills such as gathering and organizing information, evaluating arguments, and supporting a thesis.

Q. How does writing enhance learning?

A. Whether the assignment is a 10-minute freewriting or a full-blown research paper, writing helps students learn by enabling them to do things like . . .

- develop and record their thoughts,
- connect and analyze their ideas,
- receive a classmate's or teacher's critique,
- revise specific points or arguments,
- take ownership for what is said and how it is said.

Q. What types of WAC activities work best?

A. WAC activities come in many types: graded or nongraded; short or long; school-based forms or workplace forms; and writing that's revised and edited or writing that isn't. For example, *Writers INC* includes about 40 forms of writing, and any one of them—from journals to research papers—could be an effective learning activity in any course. In addition, pages 72-74 in this guide have activities designed for specific courses. The best activity is one that helps students achieve the course's learning goals.

Q. To grade or not to grade?

A. Teachers choose whether and how to grade an assignment by considering issues such as the course goals, the assignment goals, the type of writing done, and the amount of time that students have to write. For ideas on how to assess all types of writing, see pages 77-97 in this guide.

Setting Up a Writing-Across-the-Curriculum Program

Writing across the curriculum (WAC) is the whole faculty's assignment—teachers and administrators alike. Therefore, the material on the following pages is addressed to the entire faculty. Use it in department or faculty meetings to discuss how to build and implement a successful WAC program.

A Formal WAC Program

Your school may have an informal, undeveloped writing-across-the-curriculum program, or a formal, more refined program. In an informal program, individual teachers decide whether to use writing and how to use it. While individuals may use writing effectively, their work is not coordinated with the work of other teachers, and the school does not provide the supportive elements of a formal program. In a formal WAC program, teachers and administrators establish a coordinated, schoolwide writing program.

Elements of a formal WAC program include

- ○ **Tools** to build a unified, schoolwide writing program: (1) a writing handbook used by all teachers and students, and available to parents; (2) a writing-skills grid showing skills taught in all grades; (3) a writing-forms framework showing types of writing emphasized in each grade; and (4) student portfolios used to store, revise, and show writing.
- ○ **Periodic Faculty-Development Workshops** on topics like designing assignments, teaching the writing process, conferencing with student writers, and evaluating writing.
- ○ **An Assessment Strategy** like "traits of effective writing" taught to all students and faculty and used in all classes.
- ○ **A Writing Center** staffed throughout the day by a writing specialist who helps students do their writing and helps teachers use writing effectively.
- ○ **Collaboration** between English teachers and other teachers regarding how to use writing as a teaching and learning tool.
- ○ **Team-Taught Courses** sponsored by two or more departments and taught by teachers from these departments.

- ○ **Parent-Teacher Communication** that includes (1) posting assignments and projects on a classroom Web site or voice-mail service; (2) holding portfolio conferences with both the parents and student; (3) offering workshops to help parents help their children with writing and reading; (4) publishing a student-written newsletter for parents.

A WAC Program with *Writers INC*

Consider how the handbook can help students learn writing skills in English class and develop those skills in other classes. Also consider how the teacher's guide can help instructors use writing as a learning tool in all courses. To make this program work, be sure that . . .

- ■ every student has a personal copy of the handbook for use in all classes,
- ■ every faculty member has a *Writers INC* handbook and a *Teacher's Guide,* and
- ■ English teachers have a *Writers INC* handbook, a *Teacher's Guide,* and a *Program Guide.*

Writing Helps Students Achieve Learning Goals

Below are five reasons why teachers want students to write. To choose the best writing activity for a course or unit, think about which concepts most closely reflect your learning goals.

1. Writing to Learn New Concepts and Ideas

Popular writing-to-learn activities are usually ungraded (see examples on pages 68-69 of this guide). The purpose is not to produce finished writing, but rather to help record one's thoughts on paper, in order to organize and refine them.

2. Writing to Share Learning

Having students share their writing lets them interact with an audience and builds a healthy learning community. The school-based forms on pages 69-70 of this guide are often used for this purpose.

3. Writing to Show Learning

The most common reason content-area teachers have for asking students to write is to show learning. For these forms of writing, see the following headings in the index of *Writers INC:* Argumentation, Cause/Effect Essay, Classification, Comparison, Contrast, Definition, Description, Essay Test, Journal Writing, Learning Logs, Note Taking, Paraphrase, Process (Explaining), and Summary.

4. Writing to Explore Personal Thoughts

Exploring personal thoughts and feelings helps students connect course content and their personal questions, ideas, and plans. For these forms of writing, see the following headings in the index of *Writers INC:* Journal Writing, Learning Logs, Personal Essay, Personal Narrative, Persuasive Essay, and Poetry Writing.

5. Writing to Plan and Complete Tasks

When assigning writing to help students plan and complete their work, teachers usually choose forms of workplace writing. These forms help students (1) organize materials, develop plans, and budget time; and (2) correspond with others regarding progress on their course work. (See pages 296-321 in *Writers INC* and page 71 in this guide.)

School-Based Writing Helps Students Learn Course Content

For example, writing a persuasive essay (pages 115-123 in *Writers INC*) helps students develop and present an argument related to a topic discussed in class. Many models of school-based forms in the handbook demonstrate writing done in courses other than English.

Workplace Writing Helps Students Plan Their Course Work

The classroom is your students' workplace, and *Writers INC* has guidelines and models for 12 forms of workplace writing to help them do their work. For example, page 319 in the handbook shows a proposal for a science project. Consider how writing it helped the students (a) develop an overview of their project, (b) organize their ideas, (c) budget their time, (d) request help, and (e) complete the project. Also, the proposal's step-by-step procedures and deadlines helped the teacher evaluate the project.

Guides, Models, and Rubrics Help Students Do Assignments

Students sometimes write poorly because they don't understand how to develop an assigned piece of writing, or how to distinguish an unfinished piece from a finished piece. Guidelines, models, and rubrics for writing help clarify what students need to do, and how to do it for the forms of school-based writing. There are guidelines and models in *Writers INC*.

For example, the cause-and-effect organizer on pages 48 and 363 of the handbook will help you show students how to organize information for a cause-and-effect essay. The assessment rubric for academic writing on page 213 will help them revise their essays. Look through the lists below to find other helpful tools.

ADDITIONAL WRITING TOOLS

	Writers INC handbook pages
Organizing Strategies:	
• cause and effect	103
• chronological	101
• classification	100
• climax, illustration	102
• comparison	103
• order of location	100
Graphic Organizers:	
• using them	120
• for writing	48-49
• for study-reading	359-363
Rubrics:	
• academic writing	213
• book review	226
• business writing	308
• expository essay	114
• fiction writing	178
• literary analysis	226
• personal essay	154
• persuasive essay	123, 198
• poetry writing	184
• research writing	284
• subject writing	166
Working with Information:	
• analyzing	442
• applying	441
• evaluating	444
• recalling	439
• synthesizing	443
• understanding	440

Writing About . . .

Special Forms of Writing:

Guides, Strategies, and Tips

Writers INC has advice to save you time and improve students' writing. For example, if students are writing a persuasive essay, teach them how to build a clear argument by first developing a thesis statement (see *Writers INC,* pages 51 and 249). It will pay dividends: (1) the papers will be stronger, and (2) you'll save hours evaluating them. Here are some other helpful tools.

Quick Guides:

Strategies:

Tips:

Checklists:

Link Writing Assignments to Course Goals and Assessment

Design a writing assignment so it is clearly linked to course goals and an assessment rubric. When presenting the assignment, point out this link and explain how students can use the assignment, the writing guidelines, and the rubric to revise and edit their work. (See "Designing a Writing Assignment" on page 75.)

WAC Resources

Add books to the faculty's professional library. For example, you could discuss the following tips offered by Don Graves in his book, *Investigate Nonfiction:*

- Students need sustained periods of time to immerse themselves in their writing in class.

- When students have opportunities for sharing sessions about their writing in progress, they generally put more effort into their work.

- Encourage students who are writing reports to work with a subject through at least two rounds of data gathering, discussing, and exploratory writing before they establish a definite form and focus for the writing.

- Give students many information-gathering experiences. Make firsthand data-gathering experiences (like interviewing and direct observation) a priority.

- Help students learn to analyze and interpret the data they gather.

"In literate society, business involves skillful writing, reading, speaking, listening, and thinking. Writing across the curriculum helps students practice the ground rules for citizenship in such a society."

—Verne Meyer

Writing-to-Learn Forms

- prove appropriate in all courses
- require no preparation or prewriting
- enhance class discussions
- sharpen listening skills when read aloud to the class
- need not be graded
- usually are not revised
- work as prewriting activities
  (See pages 43-45 in *Writers INC*.)

In the broad sense, any writing activity (from an ungraded admit slip to a long research paper) is a form of writing to learn, because students learn about their topic while writing. However, this *Teacher's Guide* uses "writing to learn" in a narrower sense—to refer to the short, informal activities listed below.

Admit Slips @ These brief pieces of writing (usually on half sheets of paper) are collected as "admission" into class. An admit slip can be a summary of last night's reading, a question about class material, a request to review a particular point, or anything else that promotes meaningful dialogue and learning. To help students focus on the day's lesson, the teacher may read several admit slips aloud.

Brainstorming @ Brainstorming is done to collect as many ideas as possible on a particular topic. Students will come away with ideas that might be used to develop a writing or discussion topic. In brainstorming, everything is written down, even if it seems to be weak or irrelevant.

Class Minutes @ One student is selected each day to keep minutes of the day's lesson (including questions and comments) to be written up for the next class. Reading and correcting these minutes serves as a review and a listening exercise.

Clustering @ Clustering begins by placing a key word (nucleus word) in the center of the page and circling it. Students then record other words related to this word. Each word is circled, and a line connects it to the closest related word. (See examples on pages 10 and 43 of *Writers INC*.)

Completions @ Students complete an open-ended sentence (provided by other students or the teacher) in as many ways as possible. Writing completions helps students to look at a subject in different ways or focus their thinking on a particular concept.

Correspondence @ One of the most valuable benefits of writing to learn is that it provides many opportunities for students to communicate with their teachers, often in a sincere, anonymous way. Teachers should set up a channel (suggestion box, special reply notes, e-mail address) that encourages students to communicate freely and honestly.

Creative Definitions @ Students are first asked to write out definitions of new words. Then they read their definitions to the class, and the group discusses which definition is most accurate. The writing and discussion help students remember the correct definitions.

Dialogues @ Students create an imaginary dialogue between themselves and a character (a public or historical figure or a character from literature). The dialogue brings to life information on the subject. (See "Playwriting," pages 174-178 in *Writers INC*.)

Dramatic Scenarios @ Students imagine themselves to be historical characters during key moments in these people's lives, and then they write dialogues that capture the moment. For example, students might put themselves in President Truman's shoes in 1945 when he decided to bomb Hiroshima; or in Rosa Lee Parks' shoes in 1955 when she refused to take a backseat on a bus in Montgomery, Alabama.

Exit Slips @ At the end of class, students write a short piece in which they summarize, evaluate, or question something about the day's lesson and then turn in their exit slips before leaving the classroom. Teachers use the exit slips to assess the success of a lesson as well as to plan a follow-up lesson.

First Thoughts @ Students write or list their immediate impressions (or what they already know) about a topic they are preparing to study. The writing helps students focus on the topic, and it serves as a reference point for measuring learning.

Focused Writing @ Writers concentrate on a single topic (or one particular aspect of a topic) and write nonstop for a time. Like brainstorming, focused writing allows students to see how much they have to say on a particular topic.

How-To Writing @ To help students clarify how to accomplish a task, they write instructions. Ideally, they then test their writing on someone who is unfamiliar with the task. (See "Writing Instructions," pages 314-315 in *Writers INC*.)

Learning Logs @ A learning log is a journal (notebook) in which students keep their notes, thoughts, and personal reactions to a subject. For examples, see pages 398-399 in *Writers INC*.

Listing @ Freely listing ideas is an effective writing-to-learn activity. Students can begin with any idea related to the subject and list thoughts and details that come to mind. Listing is a useful quick review or progress check.

Nutshells @ The teacher stops class activity and asks students a question like this: "In a nutshell, what is the meaning or importance of the concept or idea that we're talking about?" Students write on the topic for 3 minutes, and then individuals share their writing. The teacher uses the writing to help the class refine its thinking on the topic.

Predicting @ Students are stopped at a key point in a lesson and asked to write what they think will happen next. This technique works well for lessons that have a strong cause-and-effect relationship.

Question of the Day @ Writers are asked to respond to a question ("What if?" or "Why?") that is important to a clear understanding of the lesson. To promote class discussion, the writing is usually read in class.

Stop 'n' Write @ At any point in a class discussion, students are asked to stop and write. The writing helps them to evaluate their understanding of the topic, to reflect on what has been said, and to question anything that may be unclear.

Student Teachers @ Students construct their own math word problems, science experiments, and discussion questions (which can be used for reviewing or testing). This writing task can replace routine end-of-the-chapter or workbook reviews with questions that students feel are worth asking.

Summing Up @ Students are asked to sum up what was covered in a particular lesson by writing about its importance, a possible result, a next step, or a general impression of the topic.

Warm-Ups @ Students write for the first 5 to 10 minutes of class—question-of-the-day, a freewriting, a focused writing, or any other appropriate activity. To begin class discussion of the day's lesson, the teacher can ask a few students to read their writing.

School-Based Writing Forms

- include traditional forms of writing taught in school
- are commonly introduced in English class
- form the basis for learning course material in all classes
- are usually revised and polished
- are collected and graded
- serve as one part of a unit or project
- are represented in *Writers INC* with guidelines and models

While each activity that follows is illustrated by an assignment for a specific course, the form can be used in any course. (Page numbers indicate the location of guidelines and models in *Writers INC*.)

Argumentation Essay (pages 195-197)
Family and Consumer Science: Write an essay of argumentation to promote a policy or practice that would help alleviate a serious health problem. Include specific, health-related details.

Book Review (pages 221-226)
Music: Review a book about a musician or type of music that you like.

Cause/Effect Essay (pages 205-207)
Political Science: Write an essay to show how the media's coverage of a political campaign impacted the results of the election.

Comparison Essay (pages 202-204)
History: Compare and contrast the contributions of two key individuals in the African American civil rights movement.

Definition Essay (pages 208-209)
Math: Write a definition of "coordinate plane."

Descriptive Essay (pages 156-157)
Science: Write an essay to describe the condition of a lifelong smoker's lungs.

Editorial (pages 188-189)
Psychology: Write an editorial to explain why health insurance policies should or should not cover treatment related to mental health.

Expository Essay (pages 109-114)
Physical Education: Research a common health problem experienced by high school students and write an essay to help readers understand what the problem is, and why it is a problem.

Eyewitness Account (pages 158-159)
Business: Describe an event that you witnessed during which a store clerk did or did not provide the help requested by a customer.

Fictionalized Journal (pages 168, 173)
Art: Choose an artist and one of his or her works of art. Research both, and then write a fictionalized journal entry in which the artist describes how he or she developed the piece.

Interactive Report (pages 435-436)
History: Using your comparison essay on two key individuals in the African American civil rights movement (see "Comparison Essay" on the previous page), write an interactive report in which you link the reader to important, related information.

Interview Report (pages 160-162)
Math: Interview a businessperson asking how he or she uses math in business, and what math courses or internships this person would recommend for students of business.

Journal (pages 144-146)
Family and Consumer Science: During the next week, keep a record of each item of food that you eat, including its related food group.

Learning Log (pages 398-399)
Math: Each Friday, write an entry in your learning log identifying a concept that you learned that week and reflecting on how that concept could help solve math problems when doing workplace activities like building a bridge, reading a gauge, measuring a pipe, etc.

Literary Analysis (pages 227-232)
Political Science: Analyze a political editorial, focusing on why the writer's argument is or is not convincing.

Multimedia Presentation (page 434)
Psychology: Write a multimedia presentation reporting on the work of an influential psycholo-gist or psychiatrist. Use the computer screen to highlight key ideas or concepts, and present the report to the class.

Opposing Ideas Essay (pages 192-194)
History: Write an essay of opposing ideas in which you present two different points of view on how historians will view President Clinton's impeachment hearings.

Paraphrase (pages 256-257)
Science: Write a one-paragraph paraphrase of the textbook's explanation of what a human liver does.

Personal Commentary (pages 190-191)
Art: Write a personal commentary on how the arts do or do not enrich life in your community.

Persuasive Essay (pages 115-123)
Government: Write an essay arguing for or against a state-financed school-voucher program.

Pet Peeve Essay (pages 186-187)
Business: Write a pet peeve essay about a marketing practice that annoys you.

Poetry (pages 179-184)
Art: Write a poem that describes a work of art and shares your feelings about it.

Problem/Solution Essay (pages 210-212)
Science: Write an essay in which you describe a problem related to gene therapy and a solution to this problem.

Profile of a Person (pages 163-165)
Business: Profile a businessperson whom you think tries to promote the welfare of his or her employees.

Research Paper (pages 244-295)
History: Write a report explaining how a river in the United States influenced the outcome of a major historical event.

Responses to Literature (pages 216-220)
Sociology: Pretend you are Willy Loman in *Death of a Salesman,* and your boss, Howard, just fired you. Write a dialogue between you and Howard in which you explain how his decision affects you.

Summary (pages 403-404)
Science: Write a summary of your textbook's explanation of photosynthesis.

Video Review (pages 450-451)
History: Watch "The Seeds of War," volume I of the documentary *World War II,* and then write a review in which you analyze how well the video identifies the economic causes of the war.

Workplace-Writing Forms

- are used to do work in business
- help in completing work in all classes
- form the basis for a workplace-writing unit in English
- can be used for tasks involved in extra-curricular activities
- are usually revised and polished
- are usually collected and graded
- serve as part of a larger unit or project
- are represented in *Writers INC* with guidelines and models

While each activity below is illustrated by an assignment for a specific course, the form can be used in any course. (Page numbers indicate the location of guidelines and models in *Writers INC*.)

Application Letter (pages 300, 305)
Physics: Write an application letter for a college-sponsored summer camp in physics. Include with your letter the proposal for your physics project, along with your project report.

Brochure (pages 316-317)
Family and Consumer Science: Create a brochure promoting a public-health issue in the community. Support your argument with current, correct information.

Complaint Letter (pages 300, 302)
Business: Choose a TV ad that you find dishonest or otherwise inappropriate. Analyze the ad and write a letter of complaint to the station manager explaining your position.

E-Mail (pages 312-313)
History: After you have chosen a topic for your speech, send me an e-mail message describing your thesis and requesting permission to proceed. I will respond via e-mail.

Informative Letter (pages 300, 303)
Physics: Write a letter in which you invite friends and family to the Science Fair, and explain how your project demonstrates one or more key principles of physics.

Instructions (pages 314-315)
Chemistry: Based on class discussion and information in your textbook, write instructions for the safe disposal of hydrochloric acid in our science lab.

Memo (pages 310-311)
History: By February 28, send me a memo reporting the progress that you and your partner are making on your History Day project.

Persuasive Letter (pages 300, 304)
Family and Consumer Science: Write a letter to a state or local official in which you argue for stricter enforcement of laws forbidding tobacco sales to minors. Support your argument with information that connects tobacco use and health problems.

Proposal (pages 318-319)
Biology: Write a proposal for your project and get my approval of the proposal before you begin work on the project.

Request Letter (pages 300-301)
Government: After you choose the government program that you will research, write a letter to the appropriate government official requesting information on your topic.

Résumé (pages 320-321)
Political Science: Research a politician you think is qualified for his or her office, and write a functional résumé that shows this person's qualifications. Be prepared to present your résumé as a report to the class.

Thank-You Letter (pages 300, 306)
Environmental Science: Send a thank-you letter to the expert you consulted for your science project. Place a copy of the letter in your portfolio.

Writing for Specific Courses

The activities that follow are designed for six areas of study: art, family and consumer science, language arts, mathematics and technology, science, and social studies. (Page numbers indicate guidelines and models in *Writers INC*.)

Arts (Music, Theater, Visual Art)

Arts in Review @ Write a review of an art exhibit, a concert, a play, a movie, or a film. For models, refer to reviews in newspapers and magazines. (See "Reviewing Videos," pages 450-451.)

Guess Who's Coming to School? @ Choose an artist whom you'd like to see perform at a school assembly. Write a letter to the principal or to the school's program committee describing the person's work and explaining why he or she should be invited to perform. (See "Persuasive Letter," pages 300 and 304.)

Have a Chair @ Select a chair to illustrate furniture design from a particular period. Then, as the builder of that chair, write an essay describing how the chair's design and construction affect its appearance and practical use. (See "Descriptive Writing," pages 156-157.)

How Do You Get Ideas? @ Write a letter to an artist, a musician, or an actor asking for information about the person's artwork or creative process. Report your findings to the class. (See "Request Letter," pages 300-301.)

Meet the Artist @ Research an artist (in music, theater, or visual arts) whose work you admire, and write an essay describing the person and the work. Then dress up as the artist and read your paper to the class. (See "Profile of a Person," pages 163-165.)

Practice Makes Perfect @ Interview an experienced visual artist, musician, actor, or dancer, focusing on how the person refines his or her skills. Present your findings as a report. (See "Interview Report," pages 160-162.)

Propose It! @ Write a proposal for your class project focusing on how the outcome will help you achieve the learning goals that you set for yourself at the beginning of the course. (See "Proposals," pages 318-319.)

Teach It! @ Choose a process learned during this course (like glazing a piece of pottery), and write a set of instructions that will help next year's students do the process. (See "Instructions," pages 314-315.)

Technology and the Arts @ Investigate some aspect of technology and the role it plays in visual art, theater, or music. Write your findings in an essay that you share with the class. (See "Expository Essay," pages 109-114.)

Welcome to This Place @ Research a famous historical site like a Gothic cathedral, the Parthenon, the Globe Theatre, or St. Peter's Basilica. Then design a brochure that advertises the historical and aesthetic appeal of the site. (See "Brochures," pages 316-317.)

Family and Consumer Science

Cents vs. Sense @ Analyze five or six TV or print ads related to patterns of eating. Then write an essay on your findings and share it with the class. (See "Writing Expository Essays," pages 105-111.)

Counting Your Bucks @ Choose an occupation that you may pursue and research your expected income. Then, based on the location of the job, assess all your living expenses including these: housing, utilities, food, clothing, retirement account, auto expenses, health insurance, life insurance, taxes. Compose your findings in a brochure that you present to the class. (See "Brochures," pages 316-317.)

Diet Log @ Maintain a diet log or journal for two weeks, noting everything that you have consumed. As part of each daily journal entry, reflect briefly on how you feel. (See "Journal Writing," pages 144-146.)

Different Viewpoints? @ Interview five students asking how their course work in family and consumer science is preparing them for a career. Then write a report on your findings. (See "Interview Report," pages 160-162.)

Marketing and Psychology @ Go to a grocery store and note the tastes (free samples), smells (deli, bakery), sights (colors, presentation of food, ads), and sounds (including music played). Then write an essay analyzing how these characteristics of the store may influence customers' shopping decisions.

Paraphrasing Lifestyles @ Read a magazine or an Internet article that describes some aspect of a healthful lifestyle. Write a paraphrase of the material and be ready to share your writing with the class. (See "Writing Paraphrases," pages 256-257.)

Proposing Your Project @ Write a proposal for your class project and get my approval of the proposal before you begin work on the project. (See "Proposals," pages 318-319.)

What's for Supper? @ Compile a cookbook of your class's favorite recipes. Distribute or sell the finished product. Consider organizing a potluck dinner featuring many of the recipes.

Language Arts

Almost True @ Write a few fictionalized journal entries in which you record a series of events that could have happened in the life of a character from a short story or a novel. As part of each entry, briefly reflect on how the event impacted the character's personality. (See "Fictionalized Journal Entry," page 173.)

Change for the Better? @ Write a story about a life-changing experience that could happen to someone you know or imagine. Be ready to share your story with the class. (See "Story Writing," pages 168-172.)

Good Stuff? @ Write your response to an assigned story or poem, and display your response on the bulletin board. (See "Responses to Literature," pages 216-220.)

Great Moments in Sports @ Re-create a glorious or not-so-glorious moment in sports. Write the piece as a news story, diary entry, letter, story, or poem. (Check the index of *Writers INC* for guidelines and a model for each form.)

Hot Spot! @ Observe (and take notes on) the action in a popular spot—cafeteria, store, restaurant, gym, etc. Write your findings in an observation report that you read to the class. (See "Descriptive Writing," pages 156-157.)

My Process @ The next time you develop a story, play, or poem, keep a record of your creative process by writing each day in your learning log. Describe your process in a brief essay. (See "Learning Logs," pages 398-399, and "Process Essay," pages 200-201.)

Say What? @ Develop a conversation between yourself and a character from one of your favorite books or movies. Then rehearse the dialogue with a friend, and read it to the class. (See "Playwriting," pages 174-177.)

Slice of Life @ Interview an elderly family member, neighbor, or acquaintance about growing up and/or working in an earlier time, and report your findings in an essay. (See "Conducting Interviews," page 330, and "Interview Report," pages 160-162.)

Writers on Writing @ Collect statements that writers have made about how and why they write. Design a brochure featuring these quotations and display it in the classroom. (See "Brochures," pages 316-317.)

You-Were-There Stories @ Write an imaginary short story based on a brief human-interest story in the newspaper. (See "Story Writing," pages 168-172.)

Mathematics and Technology

Backed into a Corner @ Keep a daily learning log in which you ask yourself a question about a significant concept discussed in class that day, and then answer the question. (See "Learning Logs," pages 398-399.)

Businesspeople on Technology @ Interview five businesspeople about how they use technology in their work. Design a brochure featuring these quotations and display it in the classroom. (See "Brochures," pages 316-317.)

Businesspeople on Writing @ Interview five businesspeople about how writing helps them do their work, and write a report on your findings. Be prepared to read the report in class. (See "Interview Report," pages 160-162.)

Defining Technology @ Write a half-page definition of a term, concept, or procedure discussed in class. (See "Essay of Definition," pages 208-209.)

Dramatic Math @ Write a dialogue between a mathematician and a student in which the mathematician shows why a math concept or procedure is important information. (See "Playwriting," pages 174-177.)

New Equipment @ Interview a key person at a local business or institution about its newest piece of equipment. Learn why the item was purchased, how it works, and how it has affected the business. Report your findings in a brief report. (See "Interview Report," pages 160-162.)

Poetic Math @ Write a poem (limerick or other form) explaining some math concept. Read the poem to the class, and display it on the bulletin board. (See "Poetry Writing," pages 179-183.)

Poster Math @ Design a poster illustrating a main idea, definition, or procedure in math. Display the poster in class.

Problem Solved @ Research the development of an invention (ink pens, personal computers, X-ray machines, etc.) designed to solve a specific problem. Write an essay on the topic and share it with the class. (See "Problem/Solution Essay," pages 210-212.)

Sports Records @ Compile a comprehensive record of statistics on a sport in your school.

Story Problems @ Create a story problem based on a concept discussed in class. Then exchange problems with a partner and solve them.

Technology—Yes or No! @ Write a dialogue between two people debating how a recent technological application will affect people. Then rehearse the script with a friend and read it to the class. (See "Playwriting," pages 174-178.)

Science

Both Sides Now @ Choose a controversial, science-related issue to present in an essay. Use a Venn diagram to identify the opposing ideas. (See "Venn Diagram," page 361, and "Essay of Opposing Ideas," pages 192-194.)

Careers @ Research a career related to a specific field of science, technology, or electronics. (See "Writing the Research Paper," pages 245-254.)

A Dark and Stormy Night @ Research an aspect of weather that interests you and write an essay showing the causes and effects of this phenomenon. (See "Cause/Effect Essay," pages 205-207.)

Dear Mr. Galileo @ In a letter to a scientist who died at least 50 years ago, explain how his or her work is impacting science today. (See "Informative Letter," pages 300 and 303.)

Great Scientists @ Using reference books, magazines, newspapers, and the Internet, research a great scientist. Then write a description of the person and his or her work. (See "Profile of a Person," pages 163-165.)

Mr. or Ms. Wizard @ Select a scientific concept (like gravity, density, or laser light) for a speech. Research the subject, write the speech, prepare props, and rehearse the presentation. (See "Planning a Speech," pages 422-430.)

Newsworthy Science @ Read and summarize an important science-related article in either a newspaper or magazine. Read your summary to the class and answer classmates' questions. (See "Writing Summaries," pages 403-404.)

Science @ Write an essay about whether there is a crisis in science education today and, if so, what should be done about it. (See "Writing Persuasive Essays," pages 115-123.)

Study Manuals @ Put together an instruction manual for a lab procedure. (See "Writing Instructions," pages 314-315.)

Social Studies

Fads and Politics @ Write an essay about a past or present fad showing its connection to social or political ideas of the time. (See "Writing Persuasive Essays," pages 115-123.)

Featuring . . . ? @ Develop a brochure that features the qualifications and job responsibilities of a local, state, or federal politician. (See "Brochures," pages 316-317.)

Fiction and Fact @ Read a novel about a significant historical event or issue. Then write a book review focusing on how the book did or did not help you understand the event or issue. (See "Writing a Book Review," pages 221-226.)

Good Causes @ Interview key people at a nonprofit agency in your community to learn how the agency contributes to community life, and write a report on your findings. (See "Interview Report," pages 160-162.)

Historical Sites @ Research the history of a building, company, church, or store, and write an essay describing its history. (See "Writing Expository Essays," pages 109-114.)

Knight Life @ Write an essay comparing and contrasting the lifestyles of knights from two different historical periods or countries. Give reasons for the similarities or differences. (See "Essay of Comparison," pages 202-204.)

Movers and Shakers @ Write an essay featuring the work of an important social thinker, spiritual leader, humanitarian, or citizens' advocate. (See "Profile of a Person," pages 163-166.)

Poetic Justice @ Select a serious issue or specific event studied in history (slavery, poverty, war, an assassination, a heroic rescue, etc.) and write about it in a poem that you share with the class. (See "Poetry Writing," pages 179-184.)

Speaking Up! @ Develop a conversation that you imagine may have taken place between two historical characters whom we have studied. Then rehearse the dialogue with a friend and read it to the class. (See "Playwriting," pages 174-178.)

To the Boats @ Imagine that you are George Washington about to lead your troops across the Delaware. Write a letter to Thomas Jefferson explaining why this action is necessary. (See "Informative Letter," pages 300 and 303.)

Designing a Writing Assignment

Students rarely take off on writing assignments—willingly at least—unless the work seems worth the effort. One way to show the work's value is to design meaningful course goals, connect the assignments to the goals, and evaluate the assignments with goal-related criteria. When students see that doing an assignment helps them achieve something valuable to you and them, they are more likely to make the effort needed to succeed.

For example, you will find an assignment below for these courses: English, math, science, and social studies. For each course, trace the connection between one of the course's goals; a writing assignment that helps students achieve the goal; and evaluation criteria that will help writers, peer editors, and the teacher.

English

Course Goal: To respond to literature by writing a variety of forms, including book reviews, literary analyses, character sketches, and freewriting assignments.

Assignment: For the next three class periods, read *Romeo and Juliet* and trace the development of a leading character (your choice). After you finish reading each act, write in your journal for 15 minutes to record and explore new information and insights that you have gained about the character (for example, behavior, motivations, or changes).

Evaluation: The writing shows that the student has (1) read the assignment, (2) identified information in the text revealing character development, and (3) reflected on what this information suggests about the character.

Math

Course Goal: To learn basic concepts or techniques of math and to understand how to use them to solve daily problems.

Assignment: Each Friday, choose one concept discussed in class during the week and explain in your journal (1) what the concept is and (2) how someone in the workplace uses that concept to do his or her work.

Evaluation: The journal entry accurately describes (1) a math concept discussed in class and (2) how the concept is used in the workplace.

Science

Course Goal: To learn how plants grow, and how scientific methods of assessment can measure that growth.

Assignment: Over several weeks, study the effects of sunlight on plant life. Working with a lab partner, do the following:

1. Plant the Wisconsin Fast Plant in the soil tray provided. (Soil in all trays is the same.)
2. Set the timer on your grow light for the number of hours and minutes stated on the tab attached to the tray. (Each team's plant will be lit for a different span of time.)
3. Each day, analyze plant health by counting leaves, measuring leaf sizes, grading leaf color, and measuring plant height.
4. After the experiment, write an essay explaining what you learned and how you learned it. (See "Cause/Effect Essay," pages 205-207.)

Evaluation: The notes and essay (1) are well organized and clear, (2) include accurate information requested in the assignment, (3) show that the writer understands factors involved in plant growth, and (4) show how scientific methods can measure plant growth.

Social Studies

Course Goal: To learn how strengths and weaknesses of the check-and-balance structure in our three branches of government affect our lives.

Assignment: The check-and-balance structure of government has strengths—like limiting the abuse of power—and weaknesses—like gridlock and inefficiency. Choose an incident caused by this structure that was discussed in class. After researching the topic, write a persuasive essay (1) describing the incident, (2) proving that it illustrates a strength or weakness of our government, and (3) showing how the incident affects people's lives. (See "Writing Persuasive Essays," pages 115-123.)

Evaluation: The essay (1) accurately describes a relevant incident, (2) proves that the incident reflects a strength or weakness in our governmental structure, and (3) shows how the incident affects people's lives.

Presenting a Writing Assignment

Students can complete any writing assignment more successfully if they know the following information about the assignment: subject, audience, purpose, form of writing, necessary prewriting, and criteria for evaluation. Based on your course goals, choose which of these items you should provide, and which the students should come up with themselves. Then present the information in an assignment form like the one below.

For example, if your goals call for writing that is prescriptive in focus and form, you may give students all the information below. However, if your goal is to have students respond freely to an idea, you may give them only a writing prompt and guidelines for evaluation. Students generate the rest of the information, and all forms of writing are acceptable—from poems to memos.

In either case, students should understand that having the information will help them in two ways: (1) it gives them a clearer view of the assignment, and (2) it saves them time while writing.

Subject:

Audience:

Purpose:

Form of Writing:

Prewriting Activities: (Prewriting is important if the assignment does not grow out of information or concepts already covered in class.)

1.

2.

Evaluation Guidelines: (Refer to checklists and guidelines in *Writers INC*.)

1.

2.

3.

4.

Assessment Strategies and Rubrics

The information in this section covers a number of areas related to assessment, including linking assessment to instruction and using rubrics to assess different modes of writing. (Reproducible copies of the 10 rubrics in the handbook are provided, as well as a descriptive-essay rubric.)

An Overview— Assessment and Instruction

"We must constantly remind ourselves that the ultimate purpose of evaluation is to enable students to evaluate themselves."

—Arthur Costa

In past decades, writing assessment was generally held to be the province of the teacher. Students turned in work—then waited to see what grades they would receive. Now it is widely recognized that learning to be a good assessor is one of the best ways to become a strong writer. In order to assess well, students must learn to recognize good writing. They must know and be able to describe the difference between writing that works and writing that does not work. Students learn to assess, generally, by going through three key steps:

1. Learning about the traits of writing by which their work—and that of others—will be assessed

2. Applying the traits to a wide variety of written texts

3. Applying the traits to their own work— first assessing it for strengths and weaknesses, then revising it as needed (See page 61 in this guide for additional information.)

Why should students be assessors?

Students who learn to be assessors also . . .

- learn to think like professional writers,
- take responsibility for their own revising, and
- make meaningful changes in their writing— instead of simply recopying a draft to make it look neater.

Role of Teachers and Students

Here is a quick summary of the kinds of activities teachers and students usually engage in while acting as assessors in the classroom.

Teachers

As assessors, teachers often engage in . . .

- roving conferences, roaming the classroom, observing students' work, and offering comments or questions that will help take students to next steps.
- one-on-one conferences, in which students are asked to come prepared with a question they need answered.
- informal comments—written or oral—in which the teacher offers a personal response or poses a reader's question.
- reading student work, using a general *teacher rating sheet* such as the one on page 81 in this guide, or an *assessment rubric* such as the ones in this guide (pages 83-93).
- tracking scores over time to calculate a final grade for a grading period.

Students

As assessors, students often engage in . . .

- reviewing scoring guides such as the checklist on page 26 in the handbook or the rubrics in this guide.
- using a *peer response sheet* such as the one on page 74 in the handbook.
- assessing and discussing written work that the teacher shares with the class.
- assessing their own work, using a scoring guide or rubric.
- compiling a portfolio and reflecting on the written work included.

Effective Assessment in the Classroom

"Good assessment starts with a vision of success."

—Arthur Costa

Good assessment gives students a sense of how they are growing as writers. It indicates to teachers which students are finding success, as well as the specific kinds of help other students may need. To ensure that assessment is working in your classroom, you should do the following things:

- Make sure ALL students know the criteria you will use to assess their writing. If you are going to use a rating sheet or rubric, provide them with copies (or refer them to the handbook).

- Give copies of rubrics or checklists to parents, too, so they can help their sons or daughters know what is expected of them.

- Make sure your instruction and assessment match. You cannot teach one thing and assess students on another—if you expect them to be successful.

- Involve students regularly in assessing . . .
  - ✔ published work from a variety of sources,
  - ✔ your work (share your writing—even if it's in unfinished draft form), and
  - ✔ their own work.

- Don't grade *everything* students write, or you'll be overwhelmed with stacks and stacks of papers to assess. Instead, you should encourage students to write *often*; then choose a few pieces to grade.

- Respond to the content *first*. Then look at the conventions. Correctness is important, but if you comment on spelling and mechanics before content, the message to the student is, "I don't care as much about what you say as I do about whether you spell everything correctly."

- Encourage students to save rough drafts and to collect pieces of work regularly in a portfolio. This type of collection gives students a broad picture of how they are progressing as writers.

- Ask students if they mind having comments written directly on their work. For some students, comments on sticky notes may seem less obtrusive.

Conducting Conferences

Conduct conferences to maintain an open line of communication with student writers at all points during the development of a piece of writing. Here are three common practices that you can employ to communicate with student writers during a writing project:

- **Desk-Side Conferences** occur when you stop at a student's desk to ask questions and make responses. Questions should be open-ended. This gives the writer "space" to talk and clarify his or her own thinking about the writing.

- **Scheduled Conferences** give you and a student a chance to meet in a more structured setting. In such a conference, a student may have a specific problem or need to discuss, or simply want you to assess his or her progress on a particular piece of writing.

Special Note: A typical conference should last from 3 to 5 minutes. Always try to praise one thing, ask an appropriate question, and/or offer one or two suggestions.

- **Small-Group Conferences** give three to five students who are at the same stage of the writing process or are experiencing the same problem a chance to meet with you. The goal of such conferences is twofold: first, to help students improve their writing and, second, to help them develop as evaluators of writing.

Formative vs. Summative Assessment

Formative assessment is ongoing and is often not linked to a letter grade or score. It may be as simple as a brief one-on-one conference or an informal review of the beginning of a student's draft to suggest possible next steps. **Summative assessment,** on the other hand, is a summing up of a student's performance. Formative assessments usually occur in the form of a comment—oral or written. Summative assessments take the form of . . .

✔ a letter grade,

✔ total points earned,

✔ a percentage score, or

✔ some combination of these.

Responding to Student Writing

Responding to Nongraded Writing

(Formative)

■ React noncritically with positive, supportive language.

■ Use marginal dialogue. Resist writing on or over the student's writing.

■ Respond whenever possible in the form of questions. Nurture curiosity through your inquiries.

■ Encourage risk taking.

Evaluating Graded Writing

(Summative)

■ Ask students to submit prewriting and rough drafts with their final drafts.

■ Scan final drafts once, focusing on the writing as a whole.

■ Reread them, this time assessing them for their adherence to previously established criteria.

■ Make marginal notations, if necessary, as you read the drafts a second time.

■ Scan the writing again and note the feedback you have given.

■ Complete your rating sheet or rubric, and, if necessary, write a summary comment.

Approaches for Assessing Writing

The most common forms of direct writing assessment (summative) are listed below.

Analytical assessment identifies the features, or traits, that characterize effective writing, and defines them along a continuum of performance from *incomplete* (the first or lowest level) through *fair* (the middle level) to *excellent* (the highest level). Many analytical scales run from a low of 1 point to a high of 5 or 6 points. This form of assessment tells students exactly where their strengths and weaknesses lie: "Your writing has strong ideas but needs work on voice," or "Your writing has powerful voice but lacks accuracy."

Mode-specific assessment is similar to analytic assessment except that the rating scales or scoring guides (rubrics) are designed specifically for particular modes of writing, such as narrative, expository, persuasive, and so on. This kind of assessment works best in a structured curriculum where students will be assigned particular forms and subjects for writing—rather than choosing their own writing topics. (See pages 83-93 in this guide for sample rubrics.)

Holistic assessment focuses on a piece of writing as a whole. Holistic assessors often use a checklist of traits to remind themselves of the kinds of characteristics they're looking for; this is called focused holistic assessment. The assessors do not, however, score traits separately, and this means that student writers do not know where they were most or least successful in their work.

Portfolio assessment gives students a chance to showcase their best writing or to document their growth as writers over time. In assembling a portfolio, students generally choose which pieces of writing they will complete and which ones they will include in their portfolios. (See page 96 in this guide for more information; also see page 35 in the handbook.)

Teacher Rating Sheet

Ideas

Fuzzy and disjointed
General, sketchy

1	2	3	4	5

Clear and focused
Rich in detail

Organization

No real lead, just dives in
Confusing order
Ideas not connected
Just stops—no conclusion

1	2	3	4	5

Great opening
Logical organization
Clear transitions
Powerful ending

Voice

Inappropriate voice
   for audience and purpose
Sounds bored by topic
Feels distant, disconnected

1	2	3	4	5

Right voice for audience
   and purpose
Enthusiastic about topic
Holds reader's attention

Word Choice

Overused, tired words
Modifier overload!
Meaning lost in unclear
   phrasing

1	2	3	4	5

Ear-catching phrases
Strong verbs, clear nouns
Well-chosen modifiers
Meaning very clear

Sentence Style

Hard to read
Bumpy—or strung out
Overlong sentences
   add to confusion

1	2	3	4	5

Easy to read aloud
Smooth, fluent
Varied sentence
   beginnings and
   lengths

Conventions

Numerous, distracting errors
Careless mistakes
Ineffective layout

1	2	3	4	5

Editorial correctness
Attention to detail
Effective layout

Assessment Rubrics

There are 11 rubrics to assess the different forms of writing covered in the handbook. Use these rubrics as indicated below:

Expository Writing

Use this rubric to assess informational writing, including expository essays, summaries, and basic reports. (See page 83.)

Personal Writing

Use this rubric to assess personal narratives and personal essays. (See page 84.)

Subject Writing

Use this rubric to assess eyewitness accounts, interview reports, profiles, case studies, and feature articles. (See page 85.)

Descriptive Writing

Use this rubric to assess descriptive essays, sensory reports, and observation reports. (See page 86.)

Fiction Writing

Use this rubric to assess short stories and play scripts. (See page 87.)

Poetry Writing

Use this rubric to assess all forms of poetry, from free verse to sonnets. (See page 88.)

Persuasive Writing

Use this rubric to assess persuasive essays, pet peeves, editorials, personal commentaries, and position papers. (See page 89.)

Academic Writing

Use this rubric to assess essays of comparison and definition; and process, cause/effect, and problem/solution essays. (See page 90.)

Writing About Literature

Use this rubric to assess book reviews and literary analyses. (See page 91.)

Research Writing

Use this rubric to assess research papers and personal research reports. (See page 92.)

Workplace Writing

Use this rubric to assess business letters, memos, proposals, and so on. (See page 93.)

Using Rubrics to Assess Writing

Before using these rubrics, you should read the following list of important points. (You should also read pages 78-80 in this guide.)

○ Each rubric lists the six traits of effective writing as explained in the handbook, pages 21-26, and as used to assess writing on many state writing-assessment tests.

○ Specific descriptors listed under each trait help you assess the writing for that trait.

○ Writing doesn't have to exhibit all of the descriptors under each trait to be effective.

○ Each rubric is based on a 5-point scale. A 5 means that the writing addresses a particular trait in a masterful way (**excellent**); a 4 means the trait has been handled well (**good**); a 3 means that the writing is average or competent (**fair**); a 2 indicates a weak handling of a trait (**poor**); and a 1 means the trait was not addressed (**incomplete**).

○ The rubrics can be used to assess works in progress and final drafts.

○ Students should know beforehand how their writing will be assessed. (They should understand the traits of effective writing.)

○ You can change each rubric as needed to meet the needs of the students and/or the requirements of the writing being assessed.

Using Rubrics as a Teaching Tool

Have students evaluate the effectiveness of published or student writing using a rubric as a basic guide. (You can use excerpts or complete pieces for these evaluating sessions.) At first, you may want students to focus on one specific trait (such as *organization*) during these sessions. Later on, you can ask them to evaluate a piece of writing for all of the traits. Have students discuss their evaluations after each session.

Assessment Rubric Expository Writing

_____ Stimulating Ideas

The writing . . .

- focuses on a specific informational subject clearly expressed in a thesis statement.
- contains specific facts, examples, or quotations to support the thesis.
- thoroughly informs readers.

_____ Logical Organization

- includes a clear beginning, a strong middle, and an effective ending.
- presents ideas in an organized manner.
- uses transitions to link sentences and paragraphs.

_____ Engaging Voice

- speaks clearly and knowledgeably.
- shows that the writer is truly interested in the subject.

_____ Original Word Choice

- explains or defines any unfamiliar terms.
- contains specific nouns and active verbs.

_____ Effective Sentence Style

- flows smoothly from one idea to the next.
- shows a variety of sentence lengths and structures.

_____ Correct, Accurate Copy

- exhibits the basic rules of writing.
- follows the format required by the teacher or follows some other effective design. (See handbook pages 30-32.)

Scoring Guide

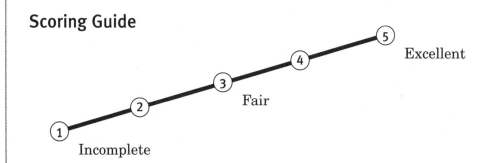

(Add any summary comments on the back of this sheet or at the bottom of the student paper.)

Assessment Rubric **Personal Writing**

_____ **Stimulating Ideas**

The writing . . .

- focuses on a specific experience or event.
- presents an engaging picture of the action and people involved.
- contains specific details and dialogue.
- makes readers want to know what happens next.

_____ **Logical Organization**

- includes a clear beginning that pulls readers into the essay.
- presents ideas in an organized manner.
- uses transitions to link sentences and paragraphs.

_____ **Engaging Voice**

- speaks knowledgeably and/or enthusiastically.
- shows that the writer is truly interested in the subject.

_____ **Original Word Choice**

- contains specific nouns, vivid verbs, and colorful modifiers.

_____ **Effective Sentence Style**

- flows smoothly from one idea to the next.
- shows variation in sentence structure and length.

_____ **Correct, Accurate Copy**

- adheres to the basic rules of writing.
- follows the form suggested by the teacher, or another effective design. (See handbook pages 30-32.)

Scoring Guide

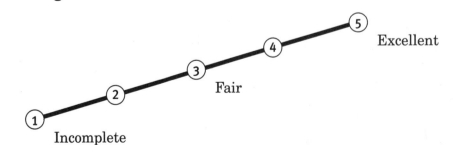

(Add any summary comments on the back of this sheet or at the bottom of the student paper.)

Assessment Rubric Subject Writing

_____ **Stimulating Ideas**

The writing . . .

- focuses on an inviting subject.
- contains a variety of supporting information (sensory details, memory details, and so on).
- informs and entertains the reader.

_____ **Logical Organization**

- includes an engaging beginning, strong development, and an effective ending.
- forms a meaningful whole, moving smoothly from one main point to the next.

_____ **Engaging Voice**

- displays a thorough knowledge of the subject.
- speaks with an appropriate voice.

_____ **Original Word Choice**

- contains specific nouns, vivid verbs, and colorful modifiers.
- captures the subject's ideas and feelings in dialogue.

_____ **Effective Sentence Style**

- flows smoothly from one idea to the next.
- shows variation in sentence structure.

_____ **Correct, Accurate Copy**

- adheres to the basic rules of grammar, spelling, and punctuation.
- follows the appropriate formatting guidelines.

Scoring Guide

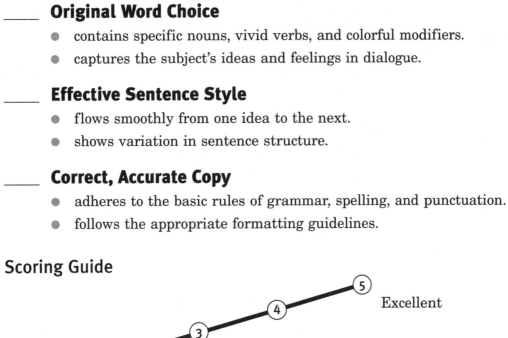

(Add any summary comments on the back of this sheet or at the bottom of the student paper.)

Assessment Rubric **Descriptive Writing**

_____ **Stimulating Ideas**

The writing . . .

- focuses on an interesting subject, object, or place.
- contains a variety of sensory details.
- informs and entertains the reader.

_____ **Logical Organization**

- has a strong beginning, clear development, and an effective ending.
- creates a whole picture of the object or place being described.

_____ **Engaging Voice**

- shows a thorough knowledge of the place or object being described.
- speaks with an appropriate voice.

_____ **Original Word Choice**

- contains specific nouns, vivid verbs, and colorful modifiers.
- uses terms appropriate to the purpose and audience.

_____ **Effective Sentence Style**

- flows smoothly from one detail to the next.
- shows a variety of sentence structure.

_____ **Correct, Accurate Copy**

- adheres to the basic rules of grammar, spelling, and punctuation.
- follows the correct formatting guidelines.

Scoring Guide

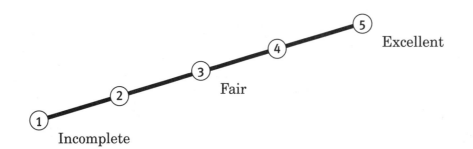

(Add any summary comments on the back of this sheet or at the bottom of the student paper.)

Assessment Rubric **Fiction Writing**

_____ Stimulating Ideas

The writing . . .

- contains an engaging setting, story line, and theme.
- brings the action alive with dialogue and details.
- develops interesting characters.

_____ Logical Organization

- follows a basic plot line, building effectively to a climax, or high point of interest. (See handbook page 239.)
- progresses in a storylike way with the characters' words and actions moving things along. (Explanations or stage directions are kept to a minimum.)

_____ Engaging Voice

- sounds realistic, in terms of the characters' dialogue.
- maintains a consistent voice for each character.

_____ Original Word Choice

- contains specific nouns, vivid verbs, and colorful modifiers.
- employs a level of language appropriate to each character.

_____ Effective Sentence Style

- flows smoothly from one idea (or line) to the next.

_____ Correct, Accurate Copy

- follows the basic rules of spelling, grammar, and punctuation.
- uses appropriate formatting guidelines for final copies.

Scoring Guide

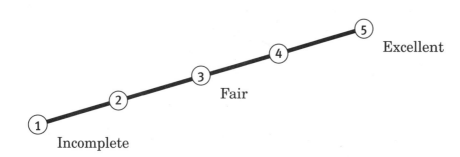

(Add any summary comments on the back of this sheet or at the bottom of the student paper.)

Assessment Rubric **Poetry Writing**

_____ Stimulating Ideas

The writing . . .

- focuses on a specific memory, feeling, belief, or person.
- brings the subject to life.
- contains strong images (word pictures).

_____ Logical Organization

- forms a meaningful whole—an idea is creatively presented and developed.
- ends with a final twist or deepening of meaning.

_____ Engaging Voice

- speaks in a voice that reflects the poem's intent.
- maintains a consistent voice throughout.

_____ Original Word Choice

- contains specific sensory details.
- employs poetic devices (metaphors, repetition, and so on).

_____ Effective Sentence Style

- moves smoothly from one image to the next.
- sounds effective when read out loud.

_____ Correct, Accurate Copy

- adheres to the basic rules of spelling and grammar.
- follows the appropriate formatting guidelines (if it is a traditional poem).
- looks interesting on the page (if it is a free-verse poem).

Scoring Guide

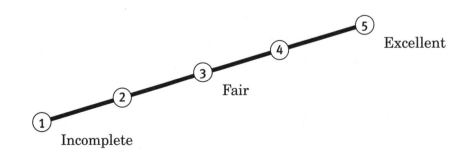

(Add any summary comments on the back of this sheet or at the bottom of the student paper.)

Assessment Rubric **Persuasive Writing**

_____ **Stimulating Ideas**

The writing . . .

- establishes an opinion or a position about a timely subject.
- contains specific facts, details, and examples to support the opinion or position.
- maintains a clear, consistent stand from start to finish.

_____ **Logical Organization**

- includes a clear beginning, strong support, and a convincing conclusion.
- arranges ideas in an organized manner (point by point; opposing arguments first, then supporting arguments; etc.).
- presents reasonable, logical arguments. (See handbook pages 118-119.)

_____ **Engaging Voice**

- speaks in a convincing and knowledgeable way.
- shows that the writer feels strongly about his or her position.

_____ **Original Word Choice**

- explains or defines any unfamiliar terms.
- uses specific nouns, vivid verbs, and convincing language.

_____ **Effective Sentence Style**

- flows smoothly from one idea to the next.
- displays varied sentence beginnings and lengths.

_____ **Correct, Accurate Copy**

- adheres to the basic rules of writing.
- follows the appropriate form and design for final copies.

Scoring Guide

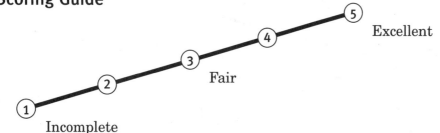

5 — Excellent
4
3 — Fair
2
1 — Incomplete

(Add any summary comments on the back of this sheet or at the bottom of the student paper.)

Assessment Rubric **Academic Writing**

_____ **Stimulating Ideas**

The writing . . .

- focuses on an important subject (a process, a problem, a term to define) that meets the requirements of the assignment.
- presents a clearly expressed thesis statement.
- thoroughly informs readers.

_____ **Logical Organization**

- includes an interesting beginning, strong development, and an effective ending.
- arranges details in a logical way. (See handbook page 52.)
- uses transitions to link sentences and paragraphs.

_____ **Engaging Voice**

- speaks knowledgeably.
- shows that the writer is truly interested in the subject.

_____ **Original Word Choice**

- explains or defines any unfamiliar terms.
- contains specific nouns and vivid verbs.

_____ **Effective Sentence Style**

- flows smoothly from one idea to the next.
- shows variation in sentence structure.

_____ **Correct, Accurate Copy**

- sticks to the basic rules of writing.
- follows the formatting requirements for the assignment.

Scoring Guide

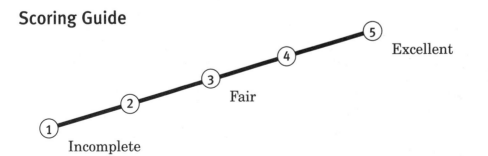

5 Excellent
4
3 Fair
2
1 Incomplete

(Add any summary comments on the back of this sheet or at the bottom of the student paper.)

Assessment Rubric Writing About Literature

____ **Stimulating Ideas**

The writing . . .

- addresses a single piece of literature (movie, performance).
- focuses on one or more important elements (plot, character, setting, or theme).
- contains supporting details and examples from the work.
- maintains a clear and consistent view from start to finish.

____ **Logical Organization**

- includes an effective beginning, strong supporting details, and a convincing conclusion.
- presents ideas in an organized manner (perhaps offering the strongest point first or last).

____ **Engaging Voice**

- speaks in a convincing and knowledgeable way.
- shows that the writer clearly understands the text.

____ **Original Word Choice**

- explains or defines any unfamiliar terms.
- pays special attention to word choice.

____ **Effective Sentence Style**

- flows smoothly from one idea to the next.

____ **Correct, Accurate Copy**

- observes the basic rules of grammar, spelling, and punctuation.
- follows the appropriate formatting guidelines.

Scoring Guide

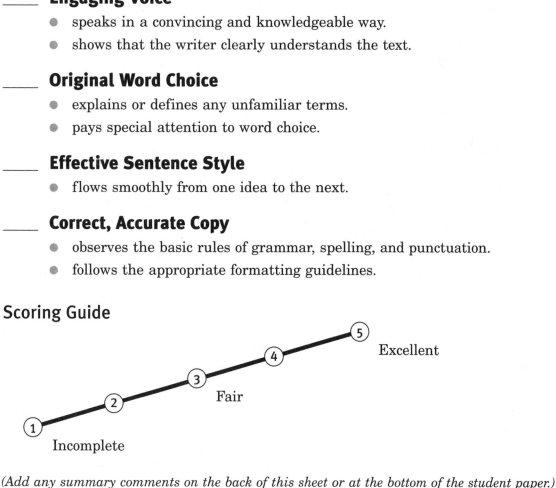

5 Excellent

4

3 Fair

2

1 Incomplete

(Add any summary comments on the back of this sheet or at the bottom of the student paper.)

Assessment Rubric Research Writing

_____ Stimulating Ideas

The writing . . .

- focuses on an important part of a subject, expressed in a thesis statement.
- effectively supports or develops the thesis with facts and details from a variety of sources.
- thoroughly informs readers.
- gives credit, when necessary, for ideas from other sources.

_____ Logical Organization

- includes a clearly developed beginning, middle, and ending.
- presents supporting information in an organized manner (one main point per paragraph).

_____ Engaging Voice

- speaks in a sincere and knowledgeable voice.
- shows that the writer is truly interested in the subject.

_____ Original Word Choice

- explains or defines any unfamiliar terms.
- employs a formal level of language.

_____ Effective Sentence Style

- flows smoothly from one idea to the next.
- shows variation in sentence structure.

_____ Correct, Accurate Copy

- adheres to the rules of grammar, spelling, and punctuation.
- follows MLA or APA guidelines for formatting and documentation.

Scoring Guide

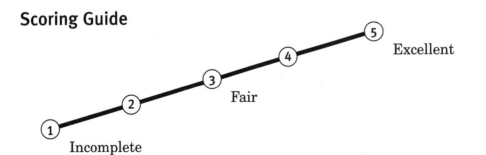

(Add any summary comments on the back of this sheet or at the bottom of the student paper.)

Assessment Rubric **Workplace Writing**

_____ **Stimulating Ideas**

The writing . . .

- focuses on an appropriate subject and format.
- develops a clearly expressed goal or purpose.

* Nicholas Davelaar writes instructions using precise details and an easy-to-follow format. (See handbook page 315.)

_____ **Logical Organization**

- includes a clear beginning, middle, and ending.
- arranges details logically using appropriate transitions.

* Adam Thoral uses headings in his résumé. (See handbook page 321.)

_____ **Engaging Voice**

- speaks knowledgeably and sincerely about the subject.

* Andrea McGrady's thank-you letter uses a friendly, informal voice to express her appreciation to her tutor. (See handbook page 306.)

_____ **Original Word Choice**

- uses plain language, specific nouns, and vivid verbs.

* Brian Krygsman's informative letter presents information clearly and uses precise Web terminology. (See handbook page 303.)

_____ **Effective Sentence Style**

- flows from one idea to the next.

* In her letter, Karin Kobes chooses transitions that lead the reader smoothly from one point to the next. (See handbook page 302.)

_____ **Correct, Accurate Copy**

- adheres to the basic rules of writing.
- follows the appropriate format.

Scoring Guide

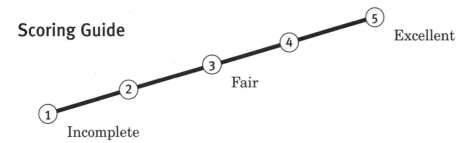

5 Excellent
4
3 Fair
2
1 Incomplete

(Add any summary comments on the back of this sheet or at the bottom of the student paper.)

Peer Response Sheet

Use a response sheet, such as the one below, to make comments about another person's writing in progress. (You may not always make responses under each category.)

Writer's Name .... Reviewer's Name ....

Title ....

I noticed . . . .

....

....

....

I liked (enjoyed, appreciated) . . . .

....

....

....

I wondered . . . .

....

....

....

I would suggest . . . .

....

....

....

Strong words, phrases, and images in the writing: ....

....

....

Peer Assessment

All writers learn to write by writing. No one questions that. But their ability to improve as writers increases significantly if they read a lot. Any writer would tell students that it is essential they become avid readers if they want to learn the craft of writing.

They would also tell students to become part of a writing community. Writers need to talk about writing with other writers. They also need to know that someone just like them—a writer writing—is available when they need help. That's why it's important that your student writers share their work throughout the process of writing. They need to feel that they are among writing colleagues—all committed to helping one another improve as writers.

A Community of Writers

The reason some teachers find the workshop approach to writing so effective is that it naturally creates a feeling of comradeship among the writers in the classroom. (See pages 56 and 62 in this guide for more information.)

The exchange of ideas among fellow writers is especially important once they have produced early drafts of their work. Writers generally get so close to their writing, so to speak, that they can't always evaluate it objectively themselves. They need their fellow writers, their peers, to ask questions, make suggestions, and offer encouragement. (Use the following minilesson as a possible starting point for group assessing.)

Peer Editing Minilesson

Provide a writing sample from a previous year for students to evaluate using the peer response sheet on page 94 in this guide.

Then discuss the strengths and weaknesses of the paper as a class after the students have finished their individual evaluations. During this discussion, make sure to tell the students how you would assess the paper and your reasons for doing so.

Types of Evaluating

There generally are three types of assessment that can go on in a peer conference. There can be a peer-revising session in which two or more student writers share ideas about a piece of writing in progress. There can be a peer-editing session in which two student writers help each other with editing a revised draft. (See the guidelines listed below for editing sessions. Also refer students to the "Editing and Proofreading Checklist," handbook page 79.) And then there are peer-assessment conferences in which fellow writers actually rate the finished pieces of writing.

Special Note: Peer assessment does not replace teacher assessment. Obviously, teachers will want to help their student writers as much as they can during the writing process. And they will want to assess the students' final products as well.

Editing Conference Guidelines

In an editing conference, a peer-editor should . . .

1. sit next to the author so that both students can see the piece of writing.
2. read the piece of writing back to the author exactly as it is written (mistakes and all).
3. allow the author to stop the reading at any time in order to edit his or her piece.
4. use a highlighting marker to point out other problems after the author has completed his or her corrections.
5. sign his or her name in the upper left-hand corner of the author's first page so that the teacher will know who helped edit the piece.

Special Note: Few peer editors are skilled enough to catch all of the mistakes in a piece of writing. Peer editors plus a teacher or a parent should always edit each piece of writing that will be assessed.

Using Writing Portfolios

> "Portfolios have become each student's story of where they are as readers and writers."
>
> —Linda Rief

More and more, English teachers are making portfolios an important part of their writing programs. Will portfolios work for you? Will they help you and your students assess their writing? Read on and find out.

Q. What is a writing portfolio?

A. A writing portfolio is a limited collection of a student's writing for evaluation. A portfolio is different from the traditional writing folder. A writing folder (also known as a working folder) contains all of a student's work; a portfolio contains only selected pieces.

There are two basic types of portfolios to create. A showcase portfolio is usually presented for evaluation at the end of a grading period. As the name implies, it should contain a selection of a student's best work. A growth portfolio notes the way in which a writer is changing and growing. This type of portfolio is usually collected regularly—say, once a month—over a long period of time.

Q. Why should I ask students to compile writing portfolios?

A. Having students compile a portfolio makes the whole process of writing more meaningful to them. They will more willingly put forth their best efforts as they work on various writing projects, knowing that they are accountable for producing a certain number of finished pieces for publication. They will more thoughtfully approach writing as an involved and recursive process of drafting, sharing, and rewriting, knowing that this process leads to more effective writing. And they will more responsibly craft finished pieces (for showcase portfolios), since their final evaluation will depend on the finished products they include in their portfolios.

Q. How many pieces of writing should be included in a portfolio?

A. Although you and your students will best be able to decide this, we advise that students compile at least three to five pieces of writing in a showcase portfolio each quarter. (The number of pieces in a growth portfolio may vary from month to month.) All of the drafts should be included for each piece. Students should also be required to include a reflective writing or self-critique sheet that assesses their writing progress.

Q. When do portfolios work best?

A. Students need plenty of class time to work on writing if they are going to produce effective portfolios. If they are used right, portfolios turn beginning writers into practicing writers. And practicing writers need regularly scheduled blocks of time to "practice" their craft, to think, talk, and explore options in their writing over and over again. Portfolios are tailor-made for language arts classrooms that operate as writing workshops.

Q. How can I help my students with their portfolio writing?

A. Allow students to explore topics of genuine interest to them. Also allow them to write for many different purposes and audiences and in many different forms.

In addition, expect students to evaluate their own writing and the writing of their peers as it develops—and help them to do so. Also provide them with sound guidance when they need help with a writing problem.

Q. How do I grade a portfolio?

A. Base each grade or assessment on goals you and your students establish beforehand and on what is achieved as evidenced in the portfolio. Many teachers develop a critique sheet for assessment based on the goals established by the class.

What About Grammar?

In the late 1980s, researchers George Hillocks, Jr., and Michael W. Smith completed a thorough study of the teaching of grammar. The purpose of their study was to determine the effectiveness of grammar instruction in school curriculums. Their research indicates that the study of grammar has no real impact on writing quality (except for the implementation of the types of activities listed on this page).

But Hillocks and Smith do point out that students need some basic understanding of grammar and mechanics to produce accurate final drafts of papers: "We assume that to proofread with any care, some knowledge of grammar must be necessary." But they go on to say that no one knows for sure what that body of knowledge is and how it is acquired.

Until such knowledge is determined, the researchers suggest that what will help student writers the most is a handy reference or guide to the rules of grammar and usage (such as the "Proofreader's Guide" in *Writers INC*).

Promoting Meaningful Grammar Instruction

The following procedures or types of activities will help students gain a better understanding of grammar and mechanics:

- Link grammar work as much as possible to the students' own writing.

- Make editing of the students' writing an important part of classroom work. They should also have practice editing and proofreading cooperatively.

- Use minilessons for grammar instruction rather than hour-long grammar activities. (See pages 111-152 in this guide.)

- Make grammar instruction fun as well as instructive. For example, develop grammar games and contests.

- Immerse students in all aspects of language learning: reading, writing, speaking, listening, and thinking. Educator James Moffett says the standard dialect is "most effectively mastered through imitating speech."

- Make sure your students understand why proper attention to standard English is important. Have experts (writers, editors, attorneys, etc.) share their thoughts on the importance of accuracy, consistency, and appropriateness in communications.

- Also make sure that your students understand what is meant by the study of grammar—the eight parts of speech, usage, agreement, and so on.

- Don't overwhelm students with too much grammar too often. Find out which skills give your students the most problems and focus your instruction accordingly.

Approaches to Use

Sentence combining—Use the students' own writing as much as possible. The rationale behind combining ideas and the proper punctuation for combining should be stressed.

Sentence expansion and revising—Offer students practice adding and changing information in sentences that they have already created. Also have them expand and revise each other's writing.

Sentence transforming—Have students change sentences from one form to another (from passive to active, beginning a sentence in a different way, using a different form of a particular word, and so on).

Sentence imitation—Students should have practice imitating writing models. According to James Moffett, this activity is a great teacher of grammar because it exposes young writers to the many possibilities of English grammar beyond the basic forms. (See page 92 in *Writers INC* for guidelines and models.)

Critical Reading Strategies

The strategies on the following pages will help you promote personalized, active reading in your classroom.

Improving Critical Reading Skills

English educators Fran Claggett, Louann Reid, and Ruth Vinz, the consulting authors of the *Daybook of Critical Reading and Writing* series (Great Source, 1999), recommend that young readers approach texts (especially fiction and poetry) in the following five ways in order to improve their critical reading skills:

1. Interact with the Text

Readers interact with a text by highlighting important or startling lines, writing notes or questions in the margins, circling words that are puzzling, or noting their reactions while reading. (Of course, if readers don't own the text, they should make all of their notations in a notebook.) By interacting with a text, readers become much more attentive and engaged in their reading and, as a result, gain more from the experience. (See page 101 in this guide for an example.)

2. Make Connections with the Text

What is happening in a text takes on more significance for readers if they make personal connections with it. The most obvious way for readers to connect with a text is to ask themselves (and try to answer) the following types of questions:

- *Have I faced a situation similar to the one faced by the main character?*
- *Have I known similar characters?*
- *Have I encountered similar problems?*
- *Would I have reacted in the same way?*
- *Do I have the same beliefs as _____?*
- *Have I read or heard about similar events?*

3. Shift Perspectives

Young readers typically think about a text in one way as they read. In other words, they take everything at face value. But if readers step back and ask themselves "what if" questions, a text often opens up in new ways for them. Here are some sample questions that can help readers see a text in new ways:

- *What if a different character told the story?*
- *What if this story took place in a different time or place?*
- *What if the main character held different beliefs?*

4. Study the Style and Craft of a Text

Writers deliberate very carefully about word choice, character development, plot development, and so on. Good critical readers constantly ask themselves questions about the writer's style and craft: *Why did the writer use that word? Why is this character introduced? Why did the story end here? Why weren't more details included about _____?* By thinking about a writer's choices, readers can better understand what the writer is trying to express.

5. Focus on a Writer's Life and Work

A writer's life often affects how he or she views the world, so gaining background information about a writer may help readers understand a text more fully. In addition, a writer's beliefs and interests become clearer by reading more than one of his or her titles.

Focusing on Nonfiction

This *think-and-learn strategy* will help readers improve their understanding of nonfiction texts.

Think BEFORE reading . . .

- Readers should ask themselves what they already know about the topic.

Think DURING reading . . .

- In a notebook they should write out questions, definitions, and important things they need to remember.

Think AFTER reading . . .

- Readers should tell themselves (or someone else) what they learned.
- They should write a summary of their reading.

(See page 364 in the handbook for more about reading nonfiction.)

Interacting with a Text

The sample page below comes from the *Daybook of Critical Reading and Writing* series (Great Source, 1999). It shows a reader interacting with a text. (In this series, students are able to make notations in their books.)

One Interactions with the Text

As you read, it is important to interact with a text, personalizing it by marking your questions and reactions. Some readers think of it as having a dialogue or conversation with the words on the page. Things you should consider doing include:

- circling any vocabulary words that you do not know
- underlining key phrases
- keeping track of the story or idea as it unfolds
- noting word patterns and repetitions or anything that strikes you as confusing or important
- writing down questions in the margins

As you read "Early in the Morning" by Li-Young Lee notice how one active reader has marked up the poem.

Response notes

Does "long grain" mean rice?

I. Description

Who: mother
father
child = poet
When: an adult looking back to childhood

Who's the speaker?

II. Commentary

Early in the Morning
Li-Young Lee

While the long grain is softening
in the water, gurgling
over a low stove flame, before
the salted Winter Vegetable is sliced
for breakfast, before the birds,
my mother glides an ivory comb
through her hair, heavy
and black as calligrapher's ink.

She sits at the foot of the bed.
My father watches, listens for
the music of the comb
against hair.

My mother combs,
pulls her hair back
tight, rolls it
around two fingers, pins it
in a bun to the back of her head.
For half a hundred years she has done this.
My father likes to see it like this.
He says it is kempt.

But I know
it is because of the way
my mother's hair falls
when he pulls the pins out.
Easily, like the curtains
when they untie them in the evening.

Insights into Critical Reading

Listed below are six categories and the types of insights that critical readers gain over time through their many reading experiences. Sharing these insights with students may help them become more insightful and skillful readers themselves.

Short Fiction

- Studying the characters helps readers connect with a story.
- Point of view—the vantage point from which a story is told—helps to determine how much readers will learn about each character.
- Knowing the basic structure of a plot leads to a more thoughtful analysis of a story.
- The description of the setting contributes to the tone or mood in a story.
- Connecting a story's theme to their own lives helps readers find deeper meaning in a story.

Poetry

- Analyzing the layout adds to an overall appreciation of a poem.
- Studying the sensory details in a poem leads to a better understanding of the poet's message or purpose.
- Exploring figures of speech deepens readers' insights into a poem.
- Studying the rhymes and/or rhythms in a poem helps readers appreciate its "music."
- Responding personally to a poem leads to better understanding.
- Noting the sound patterns—*alliteration, repetition,* etc.—in a poem gives readers insights into its tone or mood.

Nonfiction

- Employing a reading strategy (such as *think and read*) connects readers more thoughtfully to a text. (See "Focusing on Nonfiction" on page 100 in this guide.)

- Sorting out the main ideas and supporting details is the basis for understanding nonfiction texts.
- Making generalizations based on the reading leads to better understanding.
- Considering causes and effects helps readers connect ideas as they read.

Persuasive Writing

- Knowing the basic structure of an argument (see pages 118-119 in the handbook) leads to a more thoughtful analysis of persuasive texts.
- Identifying the writer's viewpoint is the starting point for analyzing and understanding a persuasive piece.
- Knowing that persuasive writers may use loaded words and stories that appeal to the emotions helps readers judge the quality of an author's argument.

Authors

- Writers draw on experiences and relationships in their own lives to create believable characters and situations in their stories.
- Writers of historical fiction blend events that happened in history with fictional details to make history come alive.
- Writers tackle tough issues to show that there are lessons to be learned from difficult situations.
- Writers use exaggeration to entertain and add humor and to give insights into the characters and their actions.

Themes

- Readers must always ask themselves "What is the writer trying to say to me?" while reading. They will know the theme when they can answer that question.
- Readers should look for additional themes beyond the primary one. These secondary themes can add to their understanding and appreciation of a text.

Thinking and Learning Strategies

The thinking and learning strategies on the following pages cover important areas often included in a complete language program.

Teaching Thinking

The market for teaching thinking was bullish at the end of the '80s, with articles regularly appearing in *Educational Leadership,* NCTE publications, and numerous other influential collections. Outstanding proponents of broader and better integrated approaches to thinking—leaders such as David Perkins, Art Costa, Richard Paul, Robin Fogarty, Barry Beyer, and others—were writing and speaking and inspiring teachers all over the country to "rethink" their classrooms.

"Believe all students can think, not just the gifted ones. Let your students know that thinking is a goal. Create the right climate and model it."
—Arthur L. Costa

Teacher Reaction

Many teachers have read and listened to what the experts have to say and, to some degree, have made thinking an important part of their curriculum.

Other teachers know that they should be challenging their students to think more critically and creatively, but they're not sure how to go about it. They wonder, in fact, if thinking is a skill that can be taught. Their concern is justified. Some educators say that effective thinking is a disposition or a temperament rather than a skill. Teachers are used to teaching skills, but teaching a disposition is another matter.

Then, of course, there are those teachers who wonder why so much fuss is being made about thinking. They say that their students have been thinking all along in their classrooms, and they're not about to change anything, thank you.

Creating a Thinking Climate in Your Classroom

For those of you who are ready to make your classrooms more "thinking oriented," we believe Arthur L. Costa offers the best advice in *Developing Minds* (ASCD, 1985). He suggests teachers teach for thinking (by creating the right classroom climate), about thinking (by helping students be more aware of their own thinking), and of thinking (by teaching thinking skills).

Teaching for Thinking

How can you create a thinking climate in your classroom? Read on and find out.

- Personalize the learning in your classroom. Students will approach learning more thoughtfully when the subject matter means something to them personally. Common sense (plus plenty of studies) tells us students won't become thoughtfully involved in work that is not relevant to them personally. What does this mean to you? Don't teach out of a textbook. Use the students' own thoughts, feelings, and interests as starting points for thinking and learning.

- Engage your students in projects. Have them produce a class newspaper or magazine. Have them write and produce a play, or a news show. Have them develop instructional manuals for skateboarding or car repair. There are any number of challenging thinking activities built into long-range projects.

- Promote activities that have heretofore been considered fillers: stories, poems, posters, letters, parodies, riddles, debates, discussions, etc. These are the types of activities that get students actively thinking and learning. (Basic skills activity sheets generally do not promote thinking.)

- Promote collaborative learning. Collaboration is at the heart of learning outside of school. We learn how to ride, fish, bake, fix, etc., with the help of friends and family members. Collaborative learning gets people actively involved, gets them thinking, and gets them learning. It should be an important element in a thinking classroom. (See "Group Skills" in *Writers INC* and "Collaborative Learning" in this guide for more information.)

HINT: Have your students work in writing groups. The give-and-take among students during writing projects promotes active thinking and better writing. (See "A Guide to Group Advising" and "A Guide to Revising" in *Writers INC* for guidelines.)

■ Promote active learning in your classroom. Give your students every opportunity to explore, take risks, and make mistakes in your classroom. Ask them open-ended questions. Initiate discussions, debates, role-playing activities, and dramatic scenarios (see pages 68-69 in this guide). Pose problems, search for alternatives, test hypotheses, and challenge your students to think and act for themselves.

Teaching About Thinking

Experts believe it's important that teachers help students think about their own thinking. Focusing on one's thinking process leads to better thinking and learning. Here are some things you can do to help students think about their own thinking.

■ Help students think about their own learning. Have them estimate how long an assignment will take, determine what materials they will need to complete an assignment, and break down challenging assignments into specific tasks. Help them find someone in class who can help them if they get stuck. Have them keep track of their progress during an extended project in a personal journal, and so on.

■ Discuss with students how the brain works. Discuss left-brain thinking versus right-brain thinking. Consider a discussion of artificial intelligence as well.

■ Select biographies of famous thinkers to share with your students.

■ Discuss with your students creative thinking, logical thinking, the connection between thinking and writing, the characteristics of effective thinkers, etc. (See the thinking skills chapter in *Writers INC* for help with this.)

■ Encourage students to take pride in their work. Remind them that their work is a reflection of their very own thinking. Have them evaluate their work upon its completion. They should consider what they liked or disliked about an assignment as well as what they succeeded at and what they need to work on. (See "Learning Logs" in *Writers INC* for more information.)

■ Remind students that it's all right to make mistakes, to get stuck, to reach dead ends. Give students an opportunity to talk or write about their thoughts and feelings when things aren't going well. Help them learn from these experiences.

■ Encourage students to connect what they have already learned to new information. Also take every opportunity to connect what they are learning to their personal lives. If you want to discuss evaluating, why not have students evaluate the merits of one pair of popular jeans versus another, of one popular pizza versus another, of one way of volunteering their services versus another?

Teaching of Thinking

A third component in a thinking classroom is direct instruction of thinking skills. Here's how to work thinking skills into your curriculum.

■ Review a taxonomy of thinking skills, and select a limited number to emphasize throughout the year—perhaps one comprehension skill (summarizing), one analyzing skill (classifying), one synthesizing skill (predicting), and one evaluating skill (persuading). (See page 438 in *Writers INC* for a list of thinking skills.)

■ Produce your own activities for instruction or use reputable thinking materials that are commercially produced.

■ Arthur Costa suggests that these skills should be not only worked into the general content area but taught independently in thinking activities. He suggests spending two or three hours per week in the direct teaching of thinking skills—until students have "mastered" these skills.

Collaborative Learning

Collaborative (cooperative) learning is a powerful classroom strategy for both teachers and students. It involves working together as we have always tried to do, but with new knowledge about group dynamics, borrowed largely from the areas of communication and psychology.

Obviously, you already know a lot about cooperative learning. You have been or are a member of many groups—families, sport teams, community groups, faculty committees, and so forth. Sometimes when we look at these groups, we tend to remember how ineffective they can be. We may have knowledge about what NOT to do. If nothing else, this is an incentive toward discovering what TO DO.

What should a teacher do?

First, we suggest that you experiment with collaborative learning before deciding if this classroom strategy is for you and your students. We provide three strategies you can use for this experimentation. The group skills you will want to work with are described in *Writers INC*.

As you experiment, keep these points in mind:

1. Collaborative learning allows teachers to move away from the front of the room and rely far less on lecturing.
2. Collaborative learning provides students with one of the most powerful ways to learn verbalization.
3. Collaborative learning gives students more ownership of their learning and therefore motivates them to become better students.

Three Strategies That Work

The three strategies you can use for experimentation follow:

Tell/Retell Groups

Application: Any reading-to-learn activity
Recommended group size: 2 (3 in one group if you have an uneven number of students)
Group skills to emphasize: Listen actively, listen accurately, and offer words of encouragement.

STEP 1: One member reads a portion of the assigned material; the second member becomes an "active listener."

STEP 2: The second member tells what he or she heard; the first member becomes the "active listener." They decide together what the essential information is. (It's okay for them to look back at the reading material.)

STEP 3: Reverse roles and read the next portion.

Smart Groups

Application: Any reading-to-learn activity
Recommended group size: 2
Group skills to emphasize: Request help or clarification when needed, offer to explain or clarify, and never use put-downs.

STEP 1: Both students read assigned material. While reading, they put a faint check mark beside each paragraph they understand and a question mark beside any sentence, word, or paragraph they do not completely understand.

STEP 2: At each question mark, team members ask for help and clarification. If they both have questions, they try together to make sense of the material. If they both agree to seek outside help, they may consult another team or the teacher. If time allows, they may share what they remember about the passages they both understand.

Up-with-Your-Head Groups

Application: Checking comprehension
Recommended group size: 4-5
Group skills to emphasize: Help a group reach a decision.

STEP 1: Ask each student to number off within each group.

STEP 2: The teacher or a panel of students asks a question about the material that has been read.

STEP 3: Each group makes sure every member in their group knows an/the answer. When the question is open-ended, the group reaches a consensus of opinion.

STEP 4: The questioner calls a number (1, 2, 3, 4, 5), and students with the corresponding number raise their hands to respond. When the question requires "the" answer, only one student need reply; but when the question is open-ended, a member from each group may reply.

Building Vocabulary

What do we know about vocabulary development?

For one thing, we know there is a strong connection between a student's vocabulary and his or her reading ability. The same is true for a student's ability to listen, speak, and write. In fact, we now recognize that each person actually has four vocabularies, one each for reading, listening, speaking, and writing (listed here from largest to smallest). Although there is much overlap, students will always be able to recognize more words than they can produce. This is important to keep in mind as you develop a program of vocabulary development for your students.

Vocabulary development must also occur across the curriculum. Students must read, hear, speak, and write with the words they are attempting to learn in their classes. Anything less and the words will not become part of their permanent "producing" vocabulary.

Existing studies tell us two things: (1) giving students lists of vocabulary words with little or no context is not an efficient way to teach vocabulary; (2) students must be actively involved with the words they are attempting to learn.

Vocabulary-Building Strategies

The following vocabulary-building strategies have taken all of these points into consideration:

Previewing in Context

1. Select 5-6 words from a chapter or selection students are about to read.
2. Have students open their books to the page and paragraph in which each word is located. Ask them to find the word, read it in context, and try to figure out the meaning.
3. Have each student write down what they think each word means.
4. Discuss possible meanings and arrive at the correct definition in this context.

Self-Collection

1. Students should set aside a portion of their journals or notebooks to collect personal vocabulary.
2. Students can collect new and interesting words from any source, preferably outside of school.
3. Each journal entry should contain the word and the context in which it was used.
4. The student can then analyze the word using its context, word parts, and dictionary definitions.

Prefix, Suffix, Root Study

1. Students should learn the most common prefixes, suffixes, and roots.
2. For a complete study of the prefixes, suffixes, and roots, students can be assigned 3-4 word parts each week for the entire year (see lists for each level on page 108 of this guide).
3. Students can be given a number of strategies for learning these word parts:

   ○ Assign students one word part daily. As you are taking roll, students can write out the word part, the definition, a sample word, and a sentence using this word, which can then be exchanged and corrected.

   ○ Students can then brainstorm for familiar words that will help them remember the meaning of each word part.

   ○ Students can be challenged to combine the word parts they have studied into as many words as possible (perhaps in 5 minutes' time, or as a challenge assignment for the next day). Special cards can also be used for this purpose.

Word Card

de	flex	ion
re		or
in	flect	ible

○ Students can also be challenged to create "new" words using the word parts they have learned. To qualify, a new word should be one that makes sense and might actually be used.

○ Students can be asked to share the "new" word and challenge other students to guess what it means and to write a sentence using this word.

○ Students can start a special section in their notebooks for word parts they come across in newspapers, magazines, and their other classes.

"Words are one of our chief means of adjusting to all situations of life. The better control we have over words, the more successful our adjustment is likely to be."

—Bergan Evans

Word Parts Study List

These lists of word parts can form the basis of a vocabulary program for levels 9, 10, and 11.

LEVEL 9

Prefixes: anti (ant), bi (bis, bin), circum (circ), deca, di, ex (e, ec, ef), hemi (demi, semi), hex, il (ir, in, im), in (il, im), intro, mono, multi, non, penta, post, pre, quad, quint, re, self, sub, super (supr), tri, un, uni

Suffixes: able (ible), ade, age, al, an (ian), ary (ery, ory), cule (ling), en, er (or), ese, ess, ful, hood, ic, id (ide), ion (sion, tion), ist, ity (ty), ize, less, ology, ship, ward

Roots: anni (annu, enni), anti, aster (astr), aud (aus), auto (aut), bibl, bio, brev, centri, chrom, chron, cide (cise), cit, clud (clus, claus), corp, crat (cracy), cred, cycl (cyclo), dem, dent (dont), derm, dict, domin, dorm, duc (duct), erg, fin, fix, flex (flect), form, fort (forc), fract (frag), geo, graph (gram), here (hes), hydr, hydra, hydro, ject, join (junct), juven, lau (lac, lot, lut), magn, mand, mania, meter, micro, migra, multi, numer, omni, ortho, ped (pod), phon, pop, port, prehend, punct, reg (recti), rupt, sci, scrib (script), serv, spec (spect, spic), sphere, tele, tempo, terra, therm, tract (tra), typ, uni, ver (veri), vid (vis), zo

LEVEL 10

Prefixes: ambi (amb), amphi, bene (bon), by, co (con, col, com), contra (counter), dia, dis (dif), eu, extra (extro), for, fore, homo, inter, mis, ob (of, op, oc), para, per, peri, poly, pro, se, sup, sus, syn (sym, sys, syl), trans (tra), ultra, under, vice

Suffixes: algia, ance (ancy), ant, ate, cian, escent, fic, fy, ish, ism, ive, ly, ment, ness, ous, some, tude

Roots: ag (agi, ig, act), anthrop, arch, aug (auc), cad (cas), cap (cip, cept), capit (capt), carn, cause (cuse, cus), ced (ceed, cede, cess), civ, clam (claim), cord (cor, cardi), cosm, crea, cresc (cret, crease, cru), deca, drome, dura, dynam, equi, fac (fact, fic, fect), fer, fid (fide, feder), gam, gen, gest, grad (gress), grat, grav, hum (human), hypn, leg, liter, log (logo, ogue, ology), luc (lum, lus, lun), man, mar (mari, mer), medi, mega, mem, mit (miss), mob (mot, mov), mon, mor (mort), nov, onym, oper, pac, pan, pater (patr), path (pathy), pend (pens, pond), phil, photo, plu (plur, plus), poli, portion, prim (prime), psych, salv (salu), sat (satis), scope, sen, sent (sens), sign (signi), sist (sta, stit), solus, solv (solu), spir, string (strict), stru (struct), tact (tang, tag, tig, ting), test, thesis (thet), tort (tors), vac, vert (vers), vict (vinc), voc, volvo

LEVEL 11

Prefixes: a (an), ab (abs, a), acro, ante, be, cata, cerebro, com, de, dys, em, en, epi, hyper, hypo, infra, intra, macro, mal, meta, miso, neo, oct, paleo, pseudo, retro, sesqui, sex (sest), suf, sug

Suffixes: cy, dom, ee, ence (ency), esis (osis), et (ette), ice, ile, ine, ite, oid, ure, y

Roots: acer (acid, acri), acu, ali (allo, alter), alt, am (amor), belli, calor, caus (caut), cognosc (gnosi), crit, cur (curs), cura, doc, don, dox, endo, fall (fals), fila (fili), flu (fluc, fluv), gastr(o), germ, gloss (glot), glu (glo), greg, helio, hema (hemo), hetero, homo, ignis, levi, liber (liver), loc (loco), loqu (locut), matri, morph, nat (nasc), neur, nom, nomen (nomin), nox (noc), pedo, pel (puls), phobia, plac, pneuma (pneumon), pon (pos, pound), proto, ri (ridi, risi), rog (roga), sacr (sanc, secr), sangui, sed (sess, sid), sequ (secu, sue), simil (simul), somnus, soph, sume (sump), ten (tin, tain), tend (tent, tens), the (theo), tom, tox, trib, tui (tuit, tut), turbo, ultima, vale (vali, valu), ven (vent), vic (vicis), viv (vita, vivi), vol, volcan (vulcan), vor

Teaching Technology Literacy

In 1974, Alvin Toffler's *Future Shock* articulated the problem of runaway technology. This problem involves more than merely adapting to rapid change. It also includes issues of technology outpacing the awareness of its implications. The Y2K bug serves as a prime example: A simple programming decision made in the 1960s could have brought the information age to a halt in the year 2000.

Further, it involves dizzying advances in information technology. Personal computers have changed the nature of information management and document production. The Internet offers an endless source of facts and opinions. Virtually anyone can publish virtually anything on the Web, and separating the wheat from the chaff is a growing challenge.

Tomorrow's students need to adapt to and master new technologies constantly. They must think on a more global scale. To solve increasingly multifaceted problems, they need to be able to work together on complex teams. Somehow, today's teachers must train students to face these challenges.

Implications for Education

These rapid advances in technology and information are bringing about a sea of change in education. Language arts educators have seen its first waves lap the shore—the shift from assigned topics to student-directed ones, the proliferation of peer collaboration, the promotion of cross-curricular projects, and the influx of new publication media. But these are only the heralds of what is to come. The focus of education is increasingly shifting to skill-based instruction, with an eye toward generating lifelong learners. As one educator has put it, our job is now to raise "a generation of free-range students."

To bring this concept sharply into focus, consider what is accomplished by teaching a student to use a particular software program. As that program becomes obsolete, so does the student's knowledge of how to use it. For students to be prepared for the future, they must learn how to master new technologies and information on a continuing basis. To update an old saying, "Give a man a fish, and you've fed him for a day. Teach a man to fish, and you've fed him until fishing conditions change."

In other words, teaching technology literacy isn't really about teaching technology at all. Rather, it is about teaching people to solve problems. Paradoxically, technology literacy is best conveyed when the technology takes a backseat to some problem-solving task. Of course, that is the role of technology in the "real world."

Technology Literacy Skills

In preparing to teach technology literacy, teachers must establish what skills will be expected of students in the future. Here is a task-based list of skills that employers, parents, and educators commonly identify.

1. Identify the Problem

For students to become self-directed, lifelong learners, they must be able to pinpoint both the problems to be solved and the knowledge to be acquired in order to intelligently set out for a solution.

2. Predict and Find Sources of Information

In order to efficiently find needed information, students must be proficient in both traditional skills, such as interviewing and library use, and electronic skills, such as accessing a database or searching the Internet.

3. Evaluate Information

With the proliferation of information sources on-line, many of them biased and misleading, critical-thinking skills are obviously more important than ever before.

4. Credit Sources

With the rapid expansion of information sources on the Internet, students must recognize their responsibility to the larger community to give proper credit for information used.

5. Formulate a Plan

Having identified and researched a problem or need, students must be able to plan a response, whether to find a solution to a problem or to report new knowledge they have acquired. Often, they will need to use information-processing technology such as spreadsheets and topic web (cluster) programs.

6. Collaborate with Others

In many cases, in order to accomplish their plans, students will need to work with peers in teams and groups of teams (often across the curriculum). They need to know how to divide the work appropriately, how to carry out their own role, and how to communicate effectively when they have information for others in the group or need information from them. It may be helpful to use resource management programs.

7. Communicate Results

When communicating information, students must be able to choose the best medium. Consequently, they must understand how to use a wide range of media, from speeches to paper reports, from electronic presentations such as video and multimedia reports to Web pages.

8. Evaluate Results

Finally, students need to judge the success of their projects, whether to recognize new needs (thus restarting the cycle) or to identify new information to apply to their next task.

Teaching Technology Literacy

Incorporating both technology and group skills into the classroom may seem a tall order. However, a few steps in the right direction are sufficient to begin, and soon technology literacy gains a momentum of its own.

Use Technology

Much of technology literacy is simply becoming comfortable with technology. Many electronic devices and programs have too many features for any one person to master them all. Instead, users learn what they need to get started, and they explore other functions later. In other words, the best way to become comfortable with new technologies is a hands-on approach.

As you explore technologies, look for ways to incorporate them into your life. For example, make it a point to use e-mail whenever possible for your communications. Make an on-line search engine your first choice for finding information. Seek out other resources on-line to make your work and personal life easier.

Use Technology in Class

As you get comfortable with these technologies, model technology literacy for your students. Share a printout of information you found on the Net. Then make sure to plan Internet access as part of the research time for student projects. Establishing and maintaining e-mail communication between teacher and students can be a great way to keep a response journal. To gain familiarity with multimedia presentations, start out by creating one of your own to use in class. Again, in doing so, you model the appropriate role of technology, as a medium for the content you wish to convey.

Work Technology into Your Assignments

Begin constructing assignments that require students to use technology for themselves. Certainly the first step is to have them use a word processor for writing papers. From there, have them work with fonts, formats, and imported graphics. Make certain that they are familiar with Web browsers. Then have them capture images from Web pages to incorporate into their papers—remembering to credit the sources. Familiarize them with an e-mail program; then have them submit an assignment as an e-mail attachment.

Multimedia projects can serve as a follow-up to an oral report. (See the handbook for details.) Eventually, incorporate task-management software into projects as well.

Let Students Experiment

Give students time to work with and explore new technologies for themselves. Avoid taking too active a role in their use of the equipment. To gain a sense of mastery, they must be in control of it, without worrying that they might break something. Bear in mind that there are few computer problems that can't be fixed by shutting down the computer and restarting it.

Build Professional Relationships

Teachers and computer professionals alike work best in an environment of mutual support. Cross-curricular projects serve as a natural spawning ground for partnerships. Many teachers are developing contacts with other teachers across the Internet, allowing their classes to communicate with one another as well.

Resources on the Web

For more information, explore the ISTE (International Society for Technology in Education) Home Page <www.iste.org>. This Web site contains many teacher resources.

Minilessons

The following pages contain more than 175 minilessons that you can use with the *Writers INC* handbook. At each grade level, the topics of the minilessons are presented in the same order that they are addressed in the handbook.

Using the Minilessons

Minilessons can transform any classroom into an active learning environment. (We define a minilesson as anything that lasts about 10 minutes and covers a single idea or a basic concept.) Minilessons can include the entire class, be individualized, or be done in cooperative learning groups. Ideally, each lesson will address a particular need—a need some students are experiencing right now. This makes learning much more meaningful and successful.

Implementation

Minilessons work very well in the writing workshop classroom. Those people who are stuck can be pulled together for 10 minutes each day until they solve their problem. Perhaps one group of students needs to know how to punctuate works-cited entries because they are finalizing research or I-Search papers. Another group of students may need practice combining sentences. And still another group needs time to develop their clustering skills. The diverse needs of students can be met by teaching them the skills they need . . . when they need to learn them.

More than 35 minilessons are included at each level. They address aspects of writing, reading, learning, and thinking covered in *Writers INC*.

Level 9 MINILESSONS

Voice Lessons .... Traits of Effective Writing

■ **READ** about "Engaging Voice" on page 24 in *Writers INC*.
WRITE a paragraph about your own experiences with dogs. Make sure your personal voice comes through. To see how well your voice can be "heard," **MIX UP** several classmates' papers and **DISTRIBUTE** them randomly. See if each student can **GUESS** whose paper he or she gets.

Looking Good .... Writing with a Computer

■ After you **READ** the chapter "Writing with a Computer," **TURN** to page 201 and **READ** the sample essay.
LIST at least three things you could do on a computer to create a clear, easy-to-follow design for this essay. Be specific; explain your ideas and how they would contribute to an effective design.
If possible, **TYPE** the essay into a computer and **MAKE** the changes you have suggested.

One Red Pen . . . . Prewriting: Listing

■ **TURN** to "Using Selecting Strategies" on page 43 in *Writers INC*.
READ "Listing."
PRETEND you've found a list on a scrap of paper in the street.
WRITE the list so that a reader knows it was written by a high school teacher.
    (You may choose a character other than a high school teacher. Ask a classmate to
    guess the character's identity from the "lost list" you write.)

Butcher, Baker, Candlestick Maker . . . . Selecting a Topic

■ **TURN** to the "Essentials of Life Checklist" on page 44 in *Writers INC*.
CHOOSE one item from each of the three columns.
MAKE UP three characters, each one associated with one of your three "essentials of
    life."
BEGIN to write a story that includes all three characters.
WRITE fast and freely for 5 to 8 minutes; then stop and jot down notes that will help
    you finish the story later.

Dear Batman: . . . . Selecting a Topic

■ **REVIEW** the list of topics for writing on page 135 in *Writers INC*.
PICK any topic that sparks your interest.
PICK any name that pops into your head.
WRITE a letter about your chosen topic to your chosen person.
INCLUDE the six parts of a letter explained on pages 298-299 in your handbook.

Unless What? . . . . Focused Freewriting

■ **READ** "Freewriting Tips" on page 45 in *Writers INC*.
WRITE the word "Unless" on a piece of paper and finish writing the sentence any
    way you can.
CONTINUE writing sentences focused on the topic you started with. After 5 minutes,
COMPARE your work with someone else who's done the same thing.

3:05, Arrived on Scene . . . . A Guide to Revising

■ **READ** "One Hot Night" on page 159 in *Writers INC*.
REVISE this account to read as if it were written by the firefighter in charge.
ASSUME that the firefighter's purpose for writing is to create an official record of the
    fire. Make your revision reflect the firefighter's voice and purpose. Feel free to
    make up some details as needed.

Mock Trial . . . . A Guide to Group Advising

■ After you **STUDY** the chapter on group advising, **PRACTICE** the skills and strategies you learned.

In a small group, **PICK** a piece of sample writing from the handbook to respond to. One group member will pretend to be the writer of the piece. The rest of you will respond to his or her work.

USE the peer response sheet on page 74.

When you finish, let the "author" **CRITIQUE** the responders. Were you too personal? Too negative? Too hesitant to offer constructive criticism? Too vague?

Boot Camp . . . . Writing Sentences

■ **STUDY** "Understanding the Basics" on page 82 in *Writers INC*.

Then, to make sure you do (understand them), **WRITE** new examples to replace all the sample sentences on the page.

LABEL the parts of your sentences, just as they are labeled in your handbook.

TRADE papers with a partner and **CHECK** each other's work.

On Topic . . . . Writing Paragraphs

■ **TURN** to the sample essay on pages 196-197 in *Writers INC*.

With a partner, **FIND** the topic sentence in each paragraph of the essay.

DISCUSS the reasons for your choices.

If you are unsure of any choice, **ASK** another classmate or your teacher for input.

A Dump . . . . Writing Paragraphs

■ **READ** about organization, or arranging details, in the chapter "Writing Paragraphs" in *Writers INC*. Focus especially on "Order of Location."

RECALL the layout of your bedroom at home.

SUPPOSE you want to describe your room to a pen pal 800 miles away.

WRITE a letter describing your bedroom, from the doorway to the farthest wall, from the ceiling to the floor, or from your bed to the farthest corners.

Full Speed Astern . . . . Writing Expository Essays

■ **STUDY** page 108 in *Writers INC*.

TURN to your handbook's section on academic writing.

CHOOSE any sample essay in the section and **WRITE** a topic outline or a sentence outline for it.

Dear Diary .... Writing with Style

■ **BROWSE** through the chapter "Writing with Style" on pages 125-132 in *Writers INC*.
IMAGINE you are somebody quite different from who you are: an astronaut, a Miss America candidate, a cab driver, a dolphin trainer, etc.
WRITE one page in a daily diary, using the style you imagine this person would have. Make the style clearly different from your own.

The Working Parts............................. Business Letters

■ **STUDY** the first business letter in the chapter on writing business letters.
LIST at least three differences between a business letter and a friendly letter.
DISCUSS the results of your work as a class.

Speaking Out .... Types of Information

■ **DO** this minilesson with a partner.
CHOOSE an issue that students in your school are concerned about—violence in schools, what they'll do after high school, or any other issue that interests you.
CREATE a survey designed to gather facts and opinions about the issue. (See the handbook index.)

Dueling Detectives............................ Using the Library

■ **DO** this minilesson with a partner.
CHOOSE a fact or statistic from history that neither of you knows. For example, you might choose the date of the stock-market crash that led to the Great Depression, a fact or date related to the Civil War, and so on.
Once you agree on a fact to find, work separately to see who can **FIND** it first in the library (not on the Internet or in a textbook).
When you finish, **COMPARE** notes about what you found and where and how you found it.

Grammar, Dahling .... Using a Dictionary

■ **READ** about the dictionary on page 346 in *Writers INC*. Reread the paragraph on "Etymology."
LOOK UP the etymology of the word "GRAMMAR" in a dictionary.
LOOK UP the etymology of the word "GLAMOUR."
WRITE a paragraph in answer to the question "What do grammar and glamour have in common?"

Croak/Cash In/Kick the Bucket .... Using a Thesaurus

■ **READ** about the thesaurus on page 348 in *Writers INC*.
CHOOSE one of the following pairs of words: live/die, give/take, build/destroy.
LOOK UP both words in a thesaurus and **STUDY** the words listed under each.
WRITE a paragraph explaining the differences you notice between the positive vocabulary words and the negative ones.

Numbers, Dates, and Names .... Using a Book

■ **REVIEW** "Using a Book" on page 349 in *Writers INC*.
TURN to the copyright page of *Writers INC*.
RECORD the ISBN number for the softcover edition of this book.
Also **RECORD** the copyright date of this book and one other piece of information from this page.

R and R............................... Study-Reading Strategies

■ Suppose you are in a Big Brother or Big Sister program and your young companion writes you a letter saying he or she is having trouble reading and remembering things in school.
REVIEW the study-reading strategies listed on pages 359-366 in *Writers INC,* looking for good advice to pass along.
WRITE a personal letter to your friend, giving your best advice for reading better and remembering more in school.

Giving Examples .... Improving Classroom Skills

■ **LOOK** at the illustration on page 383 in *Writers INC*. Do you know the Greek myth to which the illustration refers?
WRITE a paragraph explaining why the story of the Trojan horse makes a good illustration for a chapter about working in groups and planning ahead. (If you don't know the story, look it up or ask a classmate to fill you in.)

In the News .... Listening and Note-Taking Skills

■ **REVIEW** "Listening and Note-Taking Skills" on pages 389-396 in *Writers INC*.
HAVE a partner read a short news story from a newspaper.
LISTEN carefully and **WRITE DOWN** the *who, when, where, what, why,* and *how* of the story.
If you don't get them all the first time, **ASK** your partner to read the story again.
TRADE roles; have your partner listen while you read.

Captain's Log.................................Learning Logs

■ **READ** the information about learning logs on pages 398-399 in *Writers INC*.
WRITE down your favorite three ways of using a learning log.

Summing It Up.................................Writing to Learn

■ **STUDY** pages 403-404 in *Writers INC*.
WRITE a summary of the information about group skills on pages 384-386.

Applying Yourself.................................Thinking Skills

■ **READ** about applying information. (See the index.)
BRAINSTORM and **LIST** ways in which you apply information outside of school.
THINK about all the things you do in a typical week that require you to apply what you know.
COMPARE lists with a classmate.

Eye on the Web.................................Viewing Skills

■ **USE** the questions and "red flags" on page 453 in *Writers INC* to **WRITE** a review of one of your favorite Web sites.
INCLUDE answers to all the "questions to ask," and **NOTE** any "red flags" you found.
Finally, **TELL** whether this critical viewing has changed your opinion of the Web site.

Comma Rules.................................Commas

■ **REVIEW** the rules about the correct use of commas on pages 457-461 in the "Proofreader's Guide."
CHOOSE two rules to study carefully.
WRITE new example sentences (at least two) for each rule you have studied. (Make sure to use commas correctly.)
DISCUSS your sentences with your classmates.

Siamese Sentences .... Semicolons

- **STUDY** the rules for the proper use of semicolons on pages 461-462 in the "Proofreader's Guide."
  Then **REFER** to "Thinking Skills" on pages 437-446 in the handbook.
  FIND two pairs of sentences that could be joined with a semicolon.
  WRITE OUT the combined sentences, punctuating them correctly.

A Snaggle-Toothed Dragon .... Hyphens

- **READ** about using a hyphen to form an adjective on page 465 in the "Proofreader's Guide."
  DRAW a mythical beast of your own creation. Make it a wild-looking, colorful creature.
  LIST six hyphenated adjectives that describe your beast.
  USE your hyphenated adjectives in a piece of writing about the beast—a poem, a paragraph, or any form you choose.

Simply Dashing .... Dashes

- **STUDY** the proper uses of the dash on page 466 in the "Proofreader's Guide."
  RECALL an exciting movie you've seen or an engaging book you've read.
  IMITATE some of the example sentences on page 466, writing about the movie or book you've chosen.
  USE dashes correctly and expressively in your imitations.

Gimme Gimme.............. Quotation Marks and Apostrophes

- **REVIEW** the rules for using quotation marks and apostrophes on pages 468 and 472-473 in the "Proofreader's Guide."
  REMEMBER a time from your childhood when you and your brothers and sisters or friends were arguing over whose toys were whose.
  WRITE the argument as you imagine it must have sounded.
  USE quotation marks and apostrophes correctly in your writing.

So to Speak .... Quotation Marks

- **STUDY** the rules for using quotation marks on page 468 in the "Proofreader's Guide."
  THINK of a distinctive word, slang or otherwise, that one of your friends always uses.
  WRITE a sentence about your friend in which you use the word in a special way.
  USE quotation marks properly to draw attention to the special use.

A Different Slant .... Italics (Underlining)

■ **READ** the information about using italics (or underlining) on page 470 in the "Proofreader's Guide."
   THINK about a favorite book, movie, or television show.
   WRITE a paragraph about it, using italics in all the ways explained in your
      handbook. If you handwrite your paragraph, use underlining; if you use a
      computer, use italics.

Test Case .... Capitalization

■ **REVIEW** the rules for capitalization on pages 475-477 in the "Proofreader's Guide."
   CHOOSE a partner.
   WRITE a paragraph, using a variety of words that should be capitalized; lowercase
      these words as a test for your partner.
   EXCHANGE paragraphs and correct each other's work.

Headroom .... Plurals

■ **REVIEW** the rules for forming plural nouns found on pages 478-479 in the "Proofreader's
Guide."
   VISUALIZE one of the rooms in your house and all the objects in it.
   LIST as many of the objects as you can remember. Beside each word on your list,
      WRITE its correct plural form.
   If in doubt about the form, **CHECK** a dictionary.

Freeze-Dried Sentences .... Abbreviations

■ **FIND** the list of common abbreviations on page 482 in the "Proofreader's Guide."
   TRANSLATE the following sentence into plain English by writing out the abbreviated
      words: R.S.V.P. to the PTA (in c/o the D.A.) or the BBB hdqrs. ASAP w/misc. lit.
      illus. about, e.g., the GNP of Russia, the IQ of VIP's, or the avg. m.p.g. of those
      w/M.A. degrees in zoology.
   MAKE UP your own sentence using a different set of abbreviations from the list.

Accomplices in Spelling .... Commonly Misspelled Words

■ **DO** this minilesson with a partner. Separately, **GO** through the list of commonly misspelled words that begins on page 485 in the "Proofreader's Guide."

CHOOSE 10 words to make up a spelling test. The words should fit these two criteria: They should be very difficult to spell, and they should be words you think you need to know how to spell.

TEST your partner on the words you chose, then have your partner **TEST** you on the words he or she chose.

CHECK your work, then **RETEST** each other on words you missed the first time.

Capital Idea .... Using the Right Word

■ Without referring to your handbook, **WRITE** sentences using all the words below correctly. (You may use more than one of the words in each sentence.)

CHECK your work by referring to "Using the Right Word" on pages 491-500 in the "Proofreader's Guide."

If you used any words incorrectly, **WRITE** new sentences using them correctly.

affect, effect	farther, further
capital, capitol	lay, lie
continual, continuous	stationary, stationery

Nouns with Class .... Abstract and Collective Nouns

■ **REVIEW** the information under the headings "Abstract Noun" and "Collective Noun" on page 501 in the "Proofreader's Guide."

LIST at least four abstract nouns on a piece of paper.

ADD at least four collective nouns to your list.

WRITE interesting sentences in which you use both your abstract and collective nouns.

Replaceable Parts .... Pronouns and Antecedents

■ **READ** about antecedents on page 503 in the "Proofreader's Guide."

LIST four common pronouns on a piece of paper.

WRITE an interesting sentence for each pronoun.

CIRCLE the pronoun and **UNDERLINE** its antecedent (if one is named) in each of your sentences.

Bursting with Verbs .... Irregular Verbs

■ **REVIEW** the chart of irregular verbs on page 509 in the "Proofreader's Guide"; then close your book.

   LIST the following verbs on a piece of paper: *burst, catch, set,* and *shake.*

   IDENTIFY the past tense and past participle form for each verb.

   OPEN your handbook to the irregular verb chart to check your work.

For Better or for Worse .... Forms of Adverbs

■ **READ** about the different forms of adverbs on page 514 in the "Proofreader's Guide."

   WRITE freely for 5 minutes, comparing yourself to a friend, an enemy, a superstar, a famous figure from history, etc.

   CIRCLE any adverbs you have used.

   CHECK with the handbook to make sure that your comparative adverbs are correctly stated.

Prepositional Poem .... Prepositions

■ **CONSULT** the list of prepositions on page 515 in the "Proofreader's Guide."

   COMPOSE a poem of at least eight lines, on any subject, in which each line begins with a different preposition.

   TRADE poems with a partner and read your poems aloud.

   DISCUSS what each poem means.

Making Connections .... Subordinating Conjunctions

■ **REVIEW** the list of subordinating conjunctions on page 516 in the "Proofreader's Guide."

   WRITE five sentences, each one including a different subordinating conjunction.

   USE the conjunctions to create either complex or compound-complex sentences.

   EXCHANGE your work with a partner and **CHECK** each other's sentences for clarity and accuracy.

Being Experts .... Subject-Verb Agreement

■ **CONSULT** the subject-verb agreement section on pages 526-528 in the "Proofreader's Guide."

   CHOOSE one agreement rule to study.

   EXPLAIN this rule to a partner.

   WRITE your own example sentence to use during your explanation.

   ALLOW your partner to ask questions during or after your explanation.

Career Choices .... Using Fair Language

■ **LIST** as many different occupations (jobs) as you can in 5 minutes.
Then **CONSULT** "Using Fair Language" on pages 529-531 in the "Proofreader's Guide" to make sure that you have not used any unfair language in your list.
MAKE changes accordingly.
DISCUSS the results of your work with your classmates.

Sign Making.. Language

■ **REVIEW** the traffic signs on page 536 in the "Student Almanac."
INVENT three new signs you think would be helpful. They can be road signs or signs that would make life safer or smoother at school, at home, at the mall, or elsewhere.
DRAW your signs. Make sure each one is the correct color and shape for the kind of information it gives.

Delete .... Editing and Proofreading Marks

■ **SEE** the editing and proofreading marks on the inside back cover of *Writers INC*.
With a partner, **EXCHANGE** papers you wrote earlier this year for any of your classes.
EDIT your partner's paper, using the proofreading marks wherever possible.
ADD a written comment that conveys your personal response to your partner's paper as a whole.

Level 10 MINILESSONS

Writing for Your Life! .... Why Write?

■ The illustration on page 1 in *Writers INC* shows a situation in which writing could be a matter of life or death.
> **IMAGINE** another situation in which writing well would be the key to survival, and imagine yourself in that situation. Be creative; your idea can be far-out fantasy or gritty reality.
> **WRITE** a very short story (one paragraph to one page) based on your idea.

Any Questions?........................... One Writer's Process

■ **REVIEW** "Prewriting" on page 10 in the chapter "One Writer's Process."
> **LOOK** closely at the cluster on this page.
> Use it to **GENERATE** and **LIST** as many additional questions about the cluster's subject as you can. If possible, **BRAINSTORM** with a partner.

Sizing Up the Situation .... Traits of Effective Writing

■ **CHOOSE** any piece of sample writing in *Writers INC*.
> **WRITE** an evaluation of the piece, telling how well the writer used the six traits of effective writing. (**REFER** to "Traits" in the index.) Write at least a couple of sentences about each trait, and give examples from the piece to support your evaluation.

Cluster Clusters ....Clustering

■ **TURN** to page 43 in *Writers INC* and find the illustration of a prewriting technique called "clustering."
> **READ** the instructions for clustering and study the example cluster.
> **CREATE** your own cluster around the nucleus word "clustering."
> **WRITE** a short essay about your own creative thinking process, using ideas stemming from the cluster you just created.

Bowling with Bonzo .... Choosing a Subject

■ **FIND** the list of descriptive topics under "Writing Topics" on page 135 in *Writers INC*.
> **PICK** one person, one place, and one thing. (*Hint:* Pick a weird combination.)
> **WRITE** a poem in which the person talks about the thing in the place. (Can you imagine what your coach [person] would say about a monkey [thing] at a bowling alley [place]?)

Needs Work .... A Guide to Drafting

■ To have some fun and remind yourself that first drafts are supposed to be imperfect, **DRAW** a diagram entitled "Human Being: First Draft."
> **USE** your imagination to **PICTURE** what a first draft of a human might look like.
> **ADD** lots of labels to explain the parts shown and their less-than-perfect arrangement.
> **KEEP** your diagram in view when you write first drafts.
> (If you enjoy this exercise, keep going; **TRY** a first draft of a dog, a cat, a cow, and other animals. You might end up with your very own *Visual Encyclopedia of First Drafts*.)

Do You See What I See? .... A Guide to Group Advising

■ In a small group, **CHOOSE** an illustration in *Writers INC* to write about. Individually, **WRITE** for about 10 minutes about the illustration.
> You may want to spend about 5 minutes drafting and about 5 minutes revising.
> > Write in any form and style you like—a short story, a poem, a profile of a person, an eyewitness account, etc.
> Have the group **RESPOND** to each person's work using the peer response sheet in your handbook.
> As time allows, **REVISE** your work to include the group's best ideas and suggestions.

Sincere Flattery .... Writing Sentences

■ **READ** about modeling sentences on page 92 in *Writers INC*.
> Then **TRY OUT** the modeling process.
> **FIND** a sentence in your favorite book or story that you think is especially powerful.
> **MODEL** it at least twice.

And Then . . . . Writing Paragraphs

■ **USE** information from your handbook's "Historical Time Line" to **WRITE** an expository paragraph with details arranged in chronological order.
> **CHOOSE** the information you want to include; just make sure that your paragraph has a topic sentence and that every sentence supports the topic sentence.

The Day I Was Born . . . . Outlining

■ **READ** the sections about outlining on page 108 in *Writers INC*.
CUT or **TEAR** a sheet of paper into 15-20 thin strips. On each of three or four strips,
WRITE a sentence about a major turning point in your life.
On the remaining strips, **WRITE** complete sentences expressing important ideas
about those turning points.
ORGANIZE the strips into outline form on the desk or table in front of you.
IMAGINE how you would use the outline to compose your own autobiography.

Your Call . . . . Writing Expository Essays

■ With a partner or small group, **USE** the assessment rubric on page 114 in *Writers INC* to
SIZE UP the sample essay on pages 112-113.
DISCUSS how the essay measures up, noting details in the essay that support your
assessments.
When you finish, **GIVE** the essay a grade.

Strategy for Success . . . . Writing Persuasive Essays

■ **THINK** of something you would like to persuade someone to think or do.
USE a graphic organizer to work out a plan for presenting and supporting your case.
(See page 120 in *Writers INC.*)

At the Movies . . . . Using Anecdotes

■ **READ** about "showing versus telling" on page 127 in *Writers INC*.
FIND a partner and take turns talking about the most recent movie that you both
have seen.
LISTEN carefully to what your partner says and **WRITE** down any examples of
showing "writing" that you hear.
COMPARE notes; then **ADD** more showing details about the movie.

Time for a Makeover . . . . Writing with Style

■ **READ** over some pieces you have written.
THINK about your writing style and how it compares to your personal style (for
example, the way you dress and wear your hair). Is it a match? Does your
writing "sound" like you look? If you want to make a better fit, which will you
adjust—your writing style or your look?
WRITE a journal entry reflecting on these questions.

Next . . . . How to . . . ?

■ **FIND** the list of expository topics under "Writing Topics," page 135 in *Writers INC*.
CHOOSE a topic from the "How to . . . " section or make up one of your own.
TELL a classmate how to do the activity.
When you're done, **DISCUSS** with the classmate how you would share these instructions with someone who doesn't speak much English, or ask the classmate to pretend not to speak much English. Then attempt to **GIVE** this person the instructions.

A Young Audience . . . . Writing Explanations

■ **FIND** the list of expository topics under "Writing Topics," page 135 in *Writers INC*.
CHOOSE a topic under "The causes of . . . ."
PRETEND you are a kindergartner and **WRITE** a kindergartner's explanation of the causes.

A Solid Case . . . . Writing to Persuade

■ **STUDY** the example persuasive paragraph in the chapter "Writing Paragraphs," pages 95-104 in *Writers INC*.
Then **SELECT** a persuasive topic from the list on page 135 in *Writers INC*.
WRITE a persuasive paragraph about this topic, using the example as your guide. (Also check the handbook index for other sections that would help you with your writing.)

Making Connections . . . . Writing Metaphorically

■ **READ** about metaphors on page 137 in *Writers INC*.
Then **REWRITE** each of the following statements using original metaphors:
The test was hard.
Fresh orange juice is great.
SHARE the results of your work.

Categories . . . . A Survey of Writing Forms

■ With a partner, **LIST** the many different kinds of writing you've done in the past year (letter to Cousin Zelda, grocery list, book report, etc.). Then **STUDY** the survey of writing forms on page 141 in *Writers INC*.
REORGANIZE your list by categorizing your writing according to the different headings in the survey.

"Happiness is . . ." . . . . Personal Responses to Literature

■ *Writers INC* contains many quotations.
    CHOOSE a favorite quotation.
    LIST a few reasons why you like the quotation.
    WRITE a note to somebody in your class explaining what the quotation means to you.

Figuratively Speaking . . . . Figures of Speech

■ **READ** closely the definitions for the different types of figures of speech listed on page 236 in *Writers INC*.
    THINK of a great athlete or musician or actor.
    WRITE three sentences about that person and his or her way of performing, using a different figure of speech in each sentence. (Be sure your figures of speech are original.)

Short Stuff . . . . Writing Paraphrases

■ **STUDY** the guidelines for writing the paraphrase on pages 256-257 in *Writers INC*.
    CHOOSE an interesting short section from one of your textbooks in a class other than English.
    PARAPHRASE your selection, following the handbook guidelines.

Working Out the Bugs . . . . Using the Internet

■ In the chapter on using the Internet, **READ** about Netiquette.
    WRITE a paragraph about one thing you find difficult or frustrating when it comes to communicating on the Net.
    EXPLAIN what the problem is, why it bothers you, and what you think should be done about it.

Mochaloco . . . . Using the Library

■ **STUDY** the information about using a dictionary on pages 346-347 in *Writers INC*.
    USE your imagination to think up a new beverage—a coffee concoction, a fruit or vegetable juice blend, etc.
    MAKE UP a name for your beverage.
    WRITE a dictionary entry for your creation, including all the types of information listed on page 346.
    SHARE your entry with classmates.

Pie, Anyone? . . . . Reading Graphics

■ **MAKE** a pie graph that shows information about your class. (**SEE** page 352 in *Writers INC* for information about pie graphs.) The graph might show the ethnic makeup of your class; methods of transportation class members use to get to school; students involved in no extracurricular activites, one activity, two activities, three or more; etc.
   ESTIMATE how large each section of your pie should be, or do the math and use a compass to make your graph accurate.

Getting to the Root . . . . Improving Vocabulary Skills

■ **TURN** to the lists of prefixes, suffixes, and roots on pages 372-381 in *Writers INC*.
   WRITE a reasonable-sounding one-sentence definition for each of the following make-believe words, after consulting the handbook lists.
      amphidictive   micromorphosteroid   similcalorizoic
      perfractacardiology   retrojectophobia   philidiocapticule
   PUT together your own words and challenge the class to write a definition for each.

Fact Check . . . . Listening and Note-Taking Skills

■ **REVIEW** the handbook chapter on listening and note-taking skills.
   USE the sample essays in your handbook's section "Persuasive Writing" to help you practice listening for fact and opinion.
   Have a partner **READ** an essay while you **LISTEN** and **JOT DOWN** facts and opinions you hear.
   Then **REVIEW** your notes with your partner to see how you did. Did you note all the important facts and opinions? Did you classify facts and opinions correctly?
   TRADE roles so your partner can practice listening.

Key Questions . . . . Test-Taking Skills

■ **DO** this minilesson with a partner. Together, **READ** the key words and sample questions on pages 406-407 in *Writers INC*.
   For each key word, **WRITE** another sample question based on information you are studying in your classes.
   Then **REPHRASE** each question as a topic sentence. (See page 408.)

Being Narrow-Minded . . . . Speech Skills

■ **STUDY** the box at the bottom of page 422 in *Writers INC*.
   START by writing down a general subject that interests you.
   NARROW the subject three times in three different ways: to focus on a specific subject for (1) an informative speech, (2) a persuasive speech, and (3) a demonstration speech.

Decisions, Decisions . . . . Commas

■ **READ** the information on page 457 in the "Proofreader's Guide" about using commas to separate adjectives.
WRITE two sentences using adjectives that need to be separated by commas and two sentences using adjectives that do not need commas.

I Came; She Left . . . . Semicolons

■ **READ** about using a semicolon to join two independent clauses on page 461 in the "Proofreader's Guide."
WRITE three pairs of simple sentences.
COMBINE each pair using a coordinating conjunction and a comma.
Then **REWRITE** them, this time using a semicolon to combine them.
SHARE your sentences with a classmate. **DISCUSS** which versions you like best, and why.

Fallout . . . . Colons

■ **READ** the model sentence on page 463 in your handbook that shows you how to use a colon to introduce a list.
SUPPOSE your locker, your knapsack, or your purse fell open and spilled its contents on the floor.
WRITE a sentence, using a colon to introduce the long list of items a passerby might see.
Then **CREATE** another original sentence using a colon in another way.

Careful . . . . Parentheses

■ **STUDY** the rules for using parentheses on page 471 in the "Proofreader's Guide."
THINK of a dangerous procedure you've carried out—rock climbing, lighting a barbecue grill, cleaning gutters, cutting open an English muffin, etc.
WRITE a paragraph instructing someone like yourself how to perform the operation safely.
PLACE appropriate warnings and cautions in parentheses.

Dear, Deer . . . . Using the Right Word

■ **REVIEW** "Using the Right Word" on pages 491-500 in the "Proofreader's Guide."
WRITE a half page about any subject you choose. In your writing, **USE** as many wrong words as you can from the list of commonly misused pairs.
EXCHANGE papers with a partner.
CORRECT each other's errors.

Ladders of Concrete .... Nouns

- Some nouns are general, some are more specific, and some are highly specific. You can form a "ladder of specification" by putting words in increasing order of concreteness. For example, mammal—biped—human—male—male rock star—Mick Jagger.

  BUILD "ladders of specificity" starting from these general terms:

  | machine | motion | group | material |

  WRITE a short paragraph using mostly words from the general end of the "ladder."

  WRITE the same paragraph, replacing the general words with your specific ones.

Stand-Ins .... Pronouns and Antecedents

- **STUDY** the section on pronouns on pages 503-506 in the "Proofreader's Guide."

  LOOK OVER the first paragraph or two in a paper you've recently completed.

  LIST each pronoun on a piece of paper. Next to it, **LIST** its antecedent. (If there is no clear antecedent, check whether the pronoun is accurately used.)

Group Study .... Pronouns

- **REVIEW** the different classes of pronouns on page 504 in the "Proofreader's Guide."

  GATHER into a group of five students.

  Member by member, **SELECT** one class of pronouns to read about.

  SHARE something you've learned about your chosen class of pronouns with the group.

Getting a Kick Out of This .... Active and Passive Voice

- **REVIEW** active voice and passive voice on page 510 in the "Proofreader's Guide."

  CHOOSE a sport that involves hitting or kicking a ball.

  WRITE a paragraph describing a moment of intense action in that sport from the point of view of one of the players; use verbs in the active voice.

  REWRITE the paragraph, describing the same action from the point of view of the ball; use verbs in the passive voice.

Adding This to That .... Verbs, Direct and Indirect Objects

- **LEARN** about transitive verbs, direct objects, and indirect objects on page 508 in the "Proofreader's Guide."

  MAKE up five weird sentences using your own combinations from the following lists:

Verbs	Indirect Objects	Direct Objects
passed	beetle	microphone
gave	kazoo	pizza
sent	hockey stick	note
awarded	mirror	sardine

In Praise of the Phrase .... Gerund, Infinitive, and Participial Phrases

■ **STUDY** the definitions of *gerund, infinitive,* and *participle* on pages 508-509 in the "Proofreader's Guide" and the information about these verbal phrases on page 520.
    READ the following short sentences:
        1. I study a map.
        2. We take a vacation.
    CONVERT each short sentence into first, a gerund phrase; second, an infinitive phrase; and third, a participial phrase.
    After doing that, **WRITE** a complete sentence for each phrase you have made.

Rubber Chicken .... Adjectives

■ **REVIEW** the information about the forms of adjectives on page 513 in the "Proofreader's Guide."
    WRITE for 5-10 minutes about your best or worst dining experience.
    EXCHANGE papers with a classmate and **CIRCLE** examples of adjectives in the superlative form in each other's work.
    CHECK the correctness of these words.

Above and Beyond .... Prepositions

■ **READ** about prepositions on page 515 in the "Proofreader's Guide."
    WRITE about the antics of a fast-moving, very persistent fly at a picnic. Keep writing until you have used at least 20 different prepositions. Then **UNDERLINE** the prepositions.

Language Review.............................. Parts of Speech

■ **FIND** the list of eight parts of speech on page 517 in the "Proofreader's Guide."
    WRITE these words (the parts of speech) across the top of a piece of paper. Then **RECORD** your favorite sentence from anywhere in *Writers INC.*
    IDENTIFY how each word is used in the sentence. (Is the first word a noun?)
    EXCHANGE your sentence with a classmate, and **CHECK** each other's work.

What a Circus! .... Types of Sentences

■ **LEARN** about the types of sentences on pages 522-523 in the "Proofreader's Guide."
    READ the model narrative paragraph on page 98 in *Writers INC.*
    NUMBER a piece of paper from 1 to 5.
    MARK each of the first five sentences in the paragraph according to its structure: simple, compound, complex, or compound-complex.

All Arranged . . . . Sentence Variety

■ **READ** about the different sentence arrangements on page 523 in the "Proofreader's Guide."

    WRITE one sentence describing something you have done in the past week.

    DECIDE which sentence arrangement your sentence uses.

    REWRITE the sentence two times, arranging it differently each time so that you end up with one example of each arrangement.

    THINK about which sentence you like best, and why.

I Disagree . . . . Getting Sentence Parts to Agree

■ **REVIEW** "Getting Sentence Parts to Agree," beginning on page 526 in the "Proofreader's Guide."

    LOOK at the illustration at the bottom of page 528.

    WRITE an anecdote based on the illustration. **MAKE UP** names for the three characters and for their team.

    MAKE several agreement errors in your sentences.

    TRADE papers with a partner and **CORRECT** the agreement errors in each other's work.

Standard Procedure . . . . Science

■ **READ** the text at the top of page 541 in the "Student Almanac."

    Why do you think the United States continues to use its own system of measurement, even though it agreed more than 25 years ago to begin changing to the metric system?

    WRITE a paragraph answering this question. Make sure to give reasons and examples to support your answer.

Level 11 MINILESSONS

What Mr. Irving Meant Was . . . . Writing as a Process

■ **CHOOSE** one of the quotations on page 8 in *Writers INC*.
IMAGINE that you are the personal assistant to the writer of the quotation.
WRITE a press release explaining what the quotation means and why it is true or relevant to good writing.

A Trip to the Sea . . . . A Guide to Prewriting

■ **READ** the introduction to the chapter "A Guide to Prewriting."
Dip into your own "sea of experience"; **BRAINSTORM** and **LIST** memories, experiences, and information that you might enjoy writing about.
CHOOSE one item on your list and **FREEWRITE** (see page 45) for a few minutes on that topic.
KEEP your list and freewriting; you may use them to help you develop future assignments.

Tracking Down the Thesis . . . . A Guide to Prewriting

■ **READ** "Forming Your Thesis Statement" on page 51 in *Writers INC*.
WRITE a thesis statement for each of the following pieces of writing: "Education Through Application" on page 189; "The Demands of Winning" on page 191; "Saving Baseball" on page 206; and "Break It to 'Em Gently" on page 209.
You may find that you can copy some thesis statements word for word from the samples; you may need to construct some thesis statements yourself, using information in the texts.

For Example . . . . A Guide to Drafting

■ **READ** "Developing the Middle" on page 56 in *Writers INC* to learn about ways to support a thesis.
CHOOSE three methods of support and **SEARCH** through some of the writing samples in your handbook to **FIND** good examples of each.
WRITE a sentence or two explaining why each text you chose is a good example.

Sparking Interest . . . . A Guide to Drafting

■ **READ** about opening or lead paragraphs on page 55 in *Writers INC*.
Then **SELECT** an essay or narrative from your writing folder.
WRITE a new opening paragraph following one of the suggestions in the handbook.

On the Run .... A Guide to Revising

- **REVISE** the sample poem "I Am" on page 182 in *Writers INC*.
  CHANGE the first line to reflect who you are.
  KEEP some words, phrases, and lines that still work well in the revised poem.
  REPLACE those that no longer fit.

Full of Hot, Humid, Stale Air .... Writing Sentences

- **BEGIN** a story with the words "It was a dark and stormy night . . . ."
  From there, **WRITE** whatever you like; just make it as flowery and wordy as you can.
      (See page 87 in *Writers INC*.) Write at least one long paragraph.
  TRADE papers with a partner and let the hot air out of each other's sentences.
  REWRITE your partner's sentences to make them simple, clear, and natural.

Capital Punishment .... Writing Paragraphs

- **TURN** to page 98 in *Writers INC*.
  READ carefully the persuasive paragraph on capital punishment.
  DRAW a line down the middle of a blank sheet of paper.
  In the left column, **LIST** the paragraph's major reasons for abolishing capital
      punishment.
  In the right column, **WRITE** a solid objection to each of the reasons in the left column.
  WRITE your reaction to what you have just done at the bottom of the page.

Know-How .... Outlining

- **SELECT** a subject that you know a lot about (basketball, blue jeans, board games, etc.).
  FOCUS on part of that subject (playing zone defense, buying designer jeans, etc.).
  WRITE a topic outline for a brief essay on your specific subject. (See page 108 in
      Writers INC for an example outline.)

A Bee-yoo-tee-ful Life .... Writing with Style

- **READ** about anecdotes on page 127 in *Writers INC*.
  THINK of an incident that had a lasting impact on you.
  WRITE an anecdote about it.
  Then **WRITE** one sentence that tells what your anecdote shows.

Maybe? I Think? .... Insecurity in Writing

■ **LEARN** about insecurity in writing on page 132 in *Writers INC*.
Then **WRITE** for 5 minutes about a topic of your choice.
INCLUDE a lot of intensifiers (really) and qualifiers (to be perfectly honest) in your writing.
EXCHANGE your writing with a classmate and **REVISE** your partner's work so it sounds more direct and confident.

Take Action! .... Passive Style

■ **READ** about passive style on page 132 in *Writers INC*.
Then **REVIEW** a piece of writing that you have just completed or are presently working on.
CHECK each of your sentences to see if it is written in the passive or active voice.
DECIDE if you want to change any passive verbs to active ones.

Honing Your Technique .... Writer's Resource

■ "If Dad hadn't shot Walt Disney in the leg, it would have been our best vacation ever." That's the first sentence of "Vacation '58," a humorous article by John Hughes. (The article inspired a hit movie called *Summer Vacation,* and Hughes ended up being a filmmaker.)
WRITE three sentences that could be the beginnings of funny stories.
USE understatement in your sentences, as Hughes did.
(See another example of understatement on page 138 in *Writers INC*.)

One Strike, You're Out .... Plagiarism

■ **READ** the comments on the meaning of plagiarism on page 256 in *Writers INC*.
SUPPOSE you were in a debate on the topic "Resolved: Students who plagiarize on a paper should automatically fail the unit."
TAKE one side or the other (pro or con) in the debate and **WRITE** a paragraph, trying to persuade the other side of your view.
ADD one fact from a published source that is not common knowledge about the subject you are debating.

In Your Own Words .... Writing Paraphrases

■ **READ** the information on writing a paraphrase on pages 256-257 in *Writers INC*.
FIND a short poem in your literature anthology or another book.
PARAPHRASE the poem using the model in your handbook as a guide.

World's Greatest Job ....Application Letter

■ **READ** the sample letter of application on page 305 in *Writers INC*.
　　SUPPOSE there is an opening for the position of "substitute teacher" to cover for your teacher when he or she is absent.
　　SUPPOSE all the others in your class are applying for the job, since there are no minimum educational requirements and the pay is phenomenal ($50/class).
　　WRITE a letter of application so convincing that you are certain to get the job.

Says Who?..............................Types of Information

■ **DO** this minilesson in a small group.
　　TALK ABOUT exactly how you would evaluate information using the five questions on page 325 in *Writers INC*. For example, how would you find out if the information was current? Where in the information source would you look for clues? What questions would you ask yourself?
　　DISCUSS all five questions in this way.
　　TAKE NOTES on good ideas you can use in the future.

Muddled and Befuddled ....Using the Library

■ **LOOK** up *confuse* in a thesaurus.
　　CHOOSE five or more synonyms for *confuse*.
　　USE all the synonyms in a poem. (Use each word in any form you like—present or past tense, noun or verb, etc.) Try to use each synonym in a way that is a good fit for its exact meaning, connotation, and sound.

SQ3R ....Study-Reading Strategies

■ **READ** about SQ3R on page 364 in *Writers INC*.
　　LIST three pluses for this reading strategy.
　　LIST one potential drawback.
　　DISCUSS SQ3R with your classmates, using your lists as a guide.

Whence They Came ....Improving Vocabulary Skills

■ **LOOK UP** these words in a dictionary that gives word origins: *berserk, canter, croissant, cynic, marathon*. Pay special attention to the words' origins.
　　Then **WRITE** a sentence using each word correctly.

Learning by Committee .... Improving Classroom Skills

■ **REVIEW** pages 384-386 in *Writers INC* and then **DISCUSS** them in a small group. Have group members **SHARE** good and bad experiences they've had in groups, ideas for making groups work, and so on.

yr spcl dctnry .... Listening and Note-Taking Skills

■ **STUDY** the guide to creating a shorthand system on page 396 in *Writers INC*.
   START your own shorthand dictionary, either an all-inclusive one or separate shorthand glossaries for each subject.
   USE a loose-leaf notebook and begin with one page for each letter.
   THINK ABOUT terms that come up often in topics you are studying.
   WRITE DOWN each term and your special shorthand for it.

Dramatic Scenarios .... Writing to Learn

■ **READ** "Dramatic Scenarios" on page 400 in *Writers INC*.
   CHOOSE a class other than your English class, whichever one interests you the most.
   CHOOSE a famous person in that field (Mozart, Einstein, Napoleon, Plato, etc.).
   READ about that person in an encyclopedia or other book.
   CHOOSE an important moment in that person's life.
   IMAGINE and then **WRITE** this person's thoughts at that crucial moment.

Testing Yourself .... Taking the Essay Test

■ **TURN** to the chapter "Test-Taking Skills" on pages 405-419 in *Writers INC*. **FOCUS** especially on the information related to essay tests.
   FIND a paragraph in one of your textbooks (other than English) that is filled with interesting information.
   READ over the paragraph several times.
   WRITE an essay test question to which the paragraph you chose would be an excellent answer.

For Example.................................. Test-Taking Skills

■ **STUDY** the material on pages 416-418 in *Writers INC* on timed writing.
   REREAD "Writing Prompt 3" at the bottom of page 418.
   MAKE a table with one column for each type of example listed (literature, history, etc.).
   LIST as many examples as you can in each column.
   Then **STAR** the examples you would use in your essay responding to this prompt.

Ad Appeal..Speech Skills

■ In the chapter "Speech Skills," **FIND** the section titled "A Closer Look at Style." **READ** the short excerpts from speeches by John F. Kennedy and notice the appeals that they exemplify.

> **FIND** a major weekly newsmagazine.
> **STUDY** the full-page advertisements in it.
> **WRITE** a list of the different appeals you detect in the ads.

Speaking Up ....Speech Skills

■ **STUDY** the chapter on speech skills on pages 421-432 in *Writers INC*.

> **CHOOSE** one of the writing samples in your handbook that you think would make a good speech.
> **WRITE** a paragraph telling why you chose this piece—why it lends itself to spoken presentation. Also **LIST** what visual aids you would add to make this a strong speech.

Oh Captain, My Captain ....Marking Your Speech

■ In the chapter "Speech Skills," **TURN** to the box presenting symbols for marking interpretation on page 430.

> **FIND** a poem in *Writers INC* or in another book.
> **SUPPOSE** you are expected to read the poem before a large audience.
> **MARK** the text of the poem with appropriate symbols for an expressive reading.
> **READ** the poem to a partner in class, following your own markings for expression.
> **DISCUSS** your reading with your partner and **REVISE** your markings accordingly.

Thinking About Aquifers ....Thinking Guidelines

■ **STUDY** the chart "Guidelines for Thinking and Writing" on page 438 in *Writers INC*.

> **LIST** the six main operations from the chart.
> **READ** the example research paper "The Ogallala: Preserving the Great American Desert" starting on page 276 in *Writers INC*.
> Under each of the six headings, **LIST** at least one thought from the paper that demonstrates that kind of thinking.

Linking Thinking . . . . Thinking Skills

■ **STUDY** the chart "Guidelines for Thinking and Writing" on page 438 in *Writers INC.*
FOCUS your attention on synthesizing.
   CHOOSE two different courses you are taking in school right now—geometry and
      history, phys. ed. and music, etc.
   FIGURE out some way of relating material from one course to material from the
      other.
   WRITE a single clear sentence stating the relationship you see.
   EXPAND upon your sentence by writing a paragraph about the connection between
      the courses.

Hopping on Board . . . . Using Evidence and Logic

■ **REVIEW** "Fallacies of Thinking" on pages 445-446 in *Writers INC.*
   SELECT one fallacy to study carefully.
   EXPLAIN what you've learned to a classmate. (Include original examples in your
      explanation.)

Dot Dot Dot . . . . Using an Ellipsis

■ **STUDY** the guidelines for using ellipses on page 456 in the "Proofreader's Guide."
   READ the persuasive paragraph on capital punishment on page 98 in your handbook.
   CONDENSE the paragraph to five lines, using ellipses correctly, as if you were quoting
      the passage in a research paper.

Separate but Equal . . . . Commas

■ **REFER** to page 457 in the "Proofreader's Guide" to learn about using commas to separate
   adjectives that equally modify the same noun.
   WRITE three original sentences, each one containing adjectives that equally modify
      the same noun.
   USE the two tests listed in the handbook to check your work.

Loud and Clear . . . . Colons

■ **THINK** of three issues about which you have strong opinions and feelings.
   WRITE one sentence about each issue.
   USE a colon for emphasis in each sentence.
   USE the example sentence at the bottom of page 462 in the "Proofreader's Guide" as
      a model.

Matching and Modeling .... Dashes

■ **FIND** four sentences containing dashes in one of your favorite magazines.
RECORD these sentences on a piece of paper.
LIST the appropriate rule in the "Proofreader's Guide" that identifies the use of the dash in each sentence. (See page 466.)
WRITE your own sentences modeled after the examples you have listed.

Being Surrounded .... Parentheses and Brackets

■ **READ** the information about parentheses and brackets on pages 471 and 474 in the "Proofreader's Guide."
WRITE a paragraph about someone you know who is special in some way.
USE parentheses at least twice. **TRADE** paragraphs with a partner.
CHOOSE two sentences from your partner's paragraph and **REWRITE** them, adding information in brackets.
LABEL each set of brackets (474.1, 474.2, or 474.3) to show what their function is.

First, Last, and In-Between .... Capitalization

■ **FIND** guidelines for capitalizing titles on page 476 in the "Proofreader's Guide."
Then **CAPITALIZE** the following titles on your own paper:
the lion in winter (play)
clan of the cave bear (book)
by the waters of babylon (short story)
Now **PUNCTUATE** the titles correctly with underlining (italics) or quotation marks.

Right Word Rap .... Using the Right Word

■ **REVIEW** "Using the Right Word" on pages 491-500 in the "Proofreader's Guide."
CREATE a memory strategy or technique to help you remember how to use one of the commonly mixed pairs of words listed in this section.
SHARE your strategy with a classmate.

N. P. O. .... Nouns

■ **STUDY** the cases of nouns explained on page 502 in the "Proofreader's Guide."
WRITE your own explanation for each of the three cases: nominative, possessive, and objective.
INCLUDE example sentences in your explanations.
CHECK your work using the handbook.

Snarl and Growl, Whistle and Howl ....Verbs

■ **READ** the quotation at the top of page 501 in the "Proofreader's Guide."
THINK about a wild animal or a weather phenomenon.
WRITE a poem of at least eight lines about it.
USE two verbs in at least three lines of your poem.

Complex Authors ....Types of Sentences

■ **STUDY** *simple, compound, complex,* and *compound-complex* sentences on pages 522-523 in the "Proofreader's Guide."
CHOOSE one article from a modern magazine of your choice.
CHOOSE one column (or one page) of copy from the article.
UNDERLINE examples of each of the four types of sentences. **USE** a different colored marker or pencil for each type (red for simple, blue for compound, green for complex, and yellow for compound-complex).
SHARE your discoveries with a classmate.

Going in Style ....Arrangement of a Sentence

■ **STUDY** *loose, balanced, periodic,* and *cumulative* sentences on page 523 in the "Proofreader's Guide."
CHOOSE an interesting article from a major newsmagazine such as *Time, Newsweek,* or *U.S. News and World Report.*
COUNT the occurrences of each type of sentence (loose, periodic, etc.) in the article.
DECIDE if one type dominates in the writer's style.
WRITE a few comments about the article, using only the dominant type of sentence you noted.

Everyone Talks, Few Listen ....Subject-Verb Agreement

■ **STUDY** subject-verb agreement on pages 526-528 in the "Proofreader's Guide."
CHOOSE a group, club, class, council, committee, troop, team, or board you belong to today or have belonged to in the past.
WRITE sentences about the duties, responsibilities, and privileges of the group as a whole and of various individual members.
USE as many indefinite pronouns as you can in the subject positions of your sentences.
CHECK your writing for subject-verb agreement.

Computing by Hand .... Language

■ **FIND** the manual alphabet and the glossary of computer terms in the "Student Almanac."

> **WRITE** a paragraph about how you feel when you see someone using sign language.
> **CHOOSE** a partner.
> **USE** hand signs to spell out a computer term from the glossary.
> **LET** your partner find the definition and read it aloud.
> **REVERSE** roles and do it again.
> **WRITE** a paragraph about how you feel when you use sign language yourself to "speak" with your partner.

Planetary Conclusions .... Science

■ **SEE** the chart of the solar system and the table labeled "Planet Profusion" on page 543 in the "Student Almanac."

> **READ** the paragraph about our solar system.
> **WRITE** your own paragraph about our solar system.
> To compose your paragraph, **STATE** and **DISCUSS** any interesting conclusions you draw from the information in the table.
> **SHARE** your finished product with a classmate.

Speaking No Evil .... Government

■ **WRITE** a paragraph explaining what it means to "plead the fifth." Make sure to **DEFINE** "the fifth" for your readers. If you need help, **SEARCH** the almanac section of your handbook for a good clue.

Level 12 MINILESSONS

Book of Wisdom .... Why Write?

- **FIND** the quotation "Writing is the most powerful means of discovery accessible to all of us throughout life" on page 1 in *Writers INC*.
  THINK about what this quotation means; then **WRITE** your own quotation about writing.
  COLLECT your class's quotations and prepare a handout, "Wisdom for Writers."

Ready to Launch .... Publishing Your Writing

- **GET OUT** the piece of your writing that you like best.
  REVIEW the chapter "Publishing Your Writing" on pages 33-39 in *Writers INC*.
  Use the information to help you **FIND** one publication (printed or on-line) that sounds like a good place to publish your favorite piece.
  PREPARE and **SUBMIT** your work.

What I Found .... Prewriting: Clustering

- **TURN TO** "Using Selecting Strategies" on page 43 in *Writers INC*.
  READ about the technique of clustering.
  FORM a cluster based on something that you find in the room where you are now sitting.
  EXPLORE one of the ideas in the cluster by freewriting for 3 to 4 minutes.

Shaping a Subject .... 5 W's of Writing

- **READ** about the 5 W's of writing on page 46 in *Writers INC*.
  Then **OPEN** one of your textbooks to any page and **JOT DOWN** the first main idea or heading that catches your eye.
  WRITE about this idea by answering the 5 W's of writing.
  SHARE the results of your work.

The Shape of Things to Come .... A Guide to Prewriting

- Quickly **READ** the sample writings that begin on pages 159, 170, and 206 in *Writers INC*.
  For each piece of writing, **CHOOSE** one type of graphic organizer shown on pages 48-49 that would have been a good prewriting tool.
  WRITE a sentence or two explaining why you chose each organizer.

The End .... A Guide to Revising

■ In the introduction to the chapter "A Guide to Revising," you learn that Ernest Hemingway rewrote one ending 27 times.

CHOOSE a short story by any professional author.

REWRITE the ending at least once. (By "the ending," we mean "how things turn out"; don't rewrite just the last sentence!) Do your best to imitate the author's voice and style so that your new ending seems "seamless."

Breaking the Rules .... Editing and Proofreading

■ Generally, writers are advised to avoid using short, choppy sentences. But Ken Taylor's pet peeve essay on page 187 in *Writers INC* is one short, choppy sentence after another.

READ the essay.

WRITE a paragraph telling what you think of it. Did Taylor have a good reason to break the rule about choppy sentences? Does his unconventional style work? Why or why not? Would the essay be better if the sentences were lengthened and smoothed out?

Like They Always Say .... Writing Sentences

■ **READ** the quotation at the top of page 83 in *Writers INC*. The writer began with a well-known expression, but ended by going in an unexpected direction. Below are the beginnings of some more well-known sayings.

COMPLETE each saying in an unexpected way that makes a statement about sentences or about writing in general. **MAKE** your sentences complete and clear.
- The best things in life are free . . .
- One picture is worth a thousand words . . .
- The more things change . . .

Paragraph Roundup .... Writing Paragraphs

■ **FIND** seven different methods of arranging details in a paragraph on pages 100-103 in *Writers INC*. Working with a partner, **FIND** another example of each method.

SEARCH textbooks, newspapers and magazines, and other sources.

WRITE DOWN where you found each paragraph; cut it out or flag it if possible.

DISCUSS with your partner the details that exhibit each paragraph's organization.

A Meta for You .... Writing with Style

■ **READ** about metaphors on page 128 in *Writers INC*.

WRITE three metaphors that describe your home and neighborhood or your school.

CHOOSE one of your metaphors to **DEVELOP** into an extended metaphor.

"I'm Revoking Your Poetic License".......... Writer's Resource

- **WRITE** a dialogue between two characters. (They can be real people, or not.)
  USE at least four terms from "Writing Terms," beginning on page 139 in *Writers INC*.
  MAKE your dialogue hilarious, outrageous, . . . or at least interesting.

Inductive Reasoning .... Writing Terms

- **READ** about inductive reasoning and deductive reasoning on page 139 in *Writers INC*.
  WRITE an inductive paragraph about a topic of your choice.
  Then **DEVELOP** a deductive paragraph for the same topic.
  DISCUSS the results.

Stellar Minds .... Prewriting: Steps in the Research Process

- **STUDY** "Prewriting: Selecting a Subject" on pages 247-251 in *Writers INC*.
  CHOOSE one of these famous astronomers:

Ptolemy	Copernicus	Galileo
Isaac Newton	Tycho Brahe	Johannes Kepler
William Herschel	Edmund Halley	Carl Sagan

  LOOK UP the astronomer you've chosen in an all-purpose encyclopedia or in an encyclopedia of astronomy.
  NOTE the following in the encyclopedia article, if they are available: an introductory outline, headlines, illustrations, questions for discussion, topics for cross-reference, a bibliography for further reading.
  WRITE down a good question about your topic that you would like to explore.

Card Games .... Taking Notes

- **READ** "Prewriting: Searching for Information" on page 250 of *Writers INC*; pay attention to "Taking Notes."
  READ a featured essay at the end of a recent issue of *Time* or *Newsweek*.
  On one 3- by 5-inch note card, **PARAPHRASE** the paragraph that best reveals the thesis of the essay.
  On another card, **QUOTE** directly the most memorable sentence in the essay. On a third card, **COMMENT** personally in response to what you've read.

From the Horse's Mouth.................... Types of Information

- **READ** about primary and secondary sources on page 324 in *Writers INC*.
  LIST some pros and cons of primary and secondary sources. (What advantages and disadvantages does each kind of source have?)
  If possible, **COMPARE** your lists with those made by classmates.

What Everyone Knows .... Avoiding Plagiarism

■ **READ** about common knowledge on page 256 in *Writers INC*. You will find this information in the discussion of plagiarism.
  FIND two pieces of information, in a text of your choice, that you consider common knowledge. **RECORD** these examples on a piece of paper.
  SHARE the results of your work during a discussion of common knowledge.

In Your Own Words .... Writing Paraphrases

■ **READ** the guidelines for writing a paraphrase on pages 256-257 in *Writers INC*.
  CHOOSE a short speech or document that was created in the 1700s or 1800s. (Possible authors include Susan B. Anthony, Frederick Douglass, Patrick Henry, Abraham Lincoln, and Tecumseh.)
  WRITE a paraphrase of the speech or document (or part of it; write about one full page).

Amusing Ourselves to Death .... Using Quoted Material

■ **READ** "Using Quoted Material" on page 258 in *Writers INC*.
  READ the following passage until you understand it:
  "Whereas television taught the magazines [like *People* and *US*] that news is nothing but entertainment, the magazines have taught television that nothing but entertainment is news. Television programs, such as 'Entertainment Tonight,' turn information about entertainers and celebrities into 'serious' cultural content, so that the circle begins to close: Both the form and content of news become entertainment."

  (Neil Postman, *Amusing Ourselves to Death,* 112)

  REWRITE the passage using ellipses (. . .) to reduce it to less than half of its original length so that only the essential ideas remain. (In shortening the passage, do not distort its meaning.)

Last Name, First Name .... MLA Documentation Style

■ **ASSEMBLE** the following information into a complete citation in a list of works cited.
  REFER to "MLA Documentation Style" for information on completing a citation.
  The source is a book whose author is Steven Levenkron. He titled his book *Treating and Overcoming Anorexia Nervosa*. The book was published in New York by Charles Scribner's Sons in 1992.

Laurel, According to Hardy .... Parenthetical References

- **STUDY** the section "Parenthetical References" on pages 260-263 in *Writers INC*. (Focus on the instructions for citing an indirect source.)

    READ this information: The artist Paul Klee told his students once that "art is exactitude winged by intuition." William Zinsser quotes Klee's comment on page 55 of his book *Writing to Learn*. Zinsser says he likes Klee's comment as a definition of good writing.

    WRITE a sentence about Zinsser in which you quote Klee's words, and cite them parenthetically as a quotation from an indirect source.

Reading Between the Lines .... Using Context

- **REVIEW** "Using Context" on pages 369-370 in *Writers INC*.

    FIND two sentences containing unfamiliar words or ideas in one of your textbooks.

    WRITE these sentences on a piece of paper and **UNDERLINE** the unfamiliar words.

    EXCHANGE sentences with one of your classmates.

    WRITE a definition for each unfamiliar word in your partner's sentences using the context clues as your guide.

    LIST the number from page 369 in *Writers INC* that helped you write your definitions.

    CHECK your work using a dictionary.

Medical Terminology 101 .... Improving Vocabulary Skills

- Medical terms sound big and impressive, but they are fairly easy to learn since they're built from a relatively small number of prefixes, suffixes, and roots.

    Below is a list of frequently used suffixes. With a partner or small group, **BRAINSTORM** and **LIST** medical terms you have heard that end with these suffixes.

-ectomy (removal)	-osis (condition, disease)
-emia (blood)	-otomy (incision of)
-itis (inflammation)	-plasty (reconstruction)
-oma (tumor)	-scopy (visual examination)

    WRITE DOWN what you think each word means.

    LOOK UP the words in a dictionary to check their spellings and meanings.

Vocabulary Pro .... Using Word Parts

- **TURN TO** the lists of prefixes, suffixes, and roots on pages 372-381 in *Writers INC*.

    LIST the following words on a piece of paper. Skip a line between each word.

    contradict   defect   postscript   recede   neologism

    DRAW a line between the word parts in each word.

    WRITE a definition using the lists of prefixes, suffixes, and roots as your guide.

    CHECK your work using a dictionary.

Why? Why? Why? .... Writing to Learn: Pointed Questions

■ **READ** about the writing-to-learn activity called "pointed questions" on page 401 in *Writers INC.*

WRITE a sentence stating what you think would be an ideal summer job.

On the next line, **WRITE** the word "Why?"

On the next line, **ANSWER** the question "Why?" in a complete sentence.

On the next line, **WRITE** "Why?" again and answer in a complete sentence.

KEEP on going this way until you can't write anymore.

Or . . . If the "summer job" question leads nowhere, try this one: **STATE** what you would buy first if you won your state's lottery tomorrow.

Why, Indeed? .... Test-Taking Skills

■ **STUDY** the material on pages 416-418 in *Writers INC* on timed writing.

Then **APPLY** the information. **CHOOSE** one of the writing prompts under "Cause and Effect . . . " on page 419.

IMAGINE that you are going to do a timed writing on the prompt.

DO the first five steps listed on page 416.

TIME yourself; see how long it takes you to do the steps.

More Power! .... Multimedia Reports

■ **READ** the quotation from Albert Einstein on page 433 in *Writers INC.*

WRITE a paragraph explaining how this quotation applies to the writing you do in school. In what ways are "you and a computer" a more powerful writing force than "you alone"?

Firm/Obstinate/Pigheaded .... Slanted Language

■ In "Fallacies of Thinking" in *Writers INC*, focus on "Slanted Language" on page 446.

RECALL the plot of a movie you've seen lately.

TELL the plot, in one short paragraph, in such a way that you communicate neither positive nor negative feelings about the movie.

RETELL the plot in language with a strong negative charge, as if you despised the movie.

RETELL the plot in a highly positive way, as if you loved the movie.

UNDERLINE the words that show emotional bias.

(TIP: Use a thesaurus to find more emotionally loaded words.)

Soda Can Found in Mummy Case! ... Using Evidence and Logic

■ **STUDY** the section "Fallacies of Thinking" on pages 445-446 in *Writers INC*.
OBTAIN a copy of a tabloid-style newspaper.
FIND an article or advertisement in the paper that you find unconvincing.
EXAMINE the logic used to sell the product or prove a point.
POINT OUT to a partner any fallacies of thinking you detect.
EXPLAIN what makes the logic false.

If You Had to ... . Punctuation Review

■ **SCAN** the rules for commas, semicolons, and quotation marks on pages 457-462 and 468 in the "Proofreader's Guide."
TRY to punctuate the following sentence so that it makes perfect sense, using two commas, one semicolon, and three sets of quotation marks:
John where Jim had used just had had used had had had had had had the teacher's approval.

All My Possessions .... Punctuation Review

■ **REVIEW** the rules for using apostrophes on pages 472-473 in the "Proofreader's Guide." Pay special attention to the rules governing the use of apostrophes to form the singular and plural possessives of nouns.
PLAN your own minilesson to teach someone else how to form the possessive forms.
TEST your minilesson out on a classmate. **ADJUST** accordingly.

And Hurry Up About It .... Dashes

■ **READ** the information about the dash on page 466 in the "Proofreader's Guide."
WRITE five sentences that are all about dashes—50-yard dashes, dashes to the all-night donut shop, or even dashes that punctuate. Each sentence should contain an example of one use of dashes explained in your handbook.
LABEL each sentence (466.1-466.5) to show how the dash is used.

All Ready, Already .... Using the Right Word

■ **REVIEW** "Using the Right Word" on pages 491-500 in the "Proofreader's Guide."
READ the samples where both (or three) terms are used in the same sentence.
PUT the book away and **COMPOSE** five sample sentences of your own, each correctly employing a different set of contrasted terms.

Advanced Language Lingo . . . . Parts of Speech

■ **WRITE** an example of each term below in a short paragraph. **TRY** it without checking your handbook.

Then **EXCHANGE** papers with a classmate and label each example you find.

CHECK your work using the "Parts of Speech" section of your handbook.

Abstract noun	Infinitive	Participle
Gerund	Intransitive verb	Pronoun and its antecedent

Loosen Up! . . . . Arrangement of a Sentence

■ **READ** about loose sentences on page 523 in the "Proofreader's Guide."

Then **IDENTIFY** two or three examples of loose sentences in a book you have read or are presently reading.

RECORD these sentences on a piece of paper, skipping two or three lines between each example.

WRITE an original sentence for each example you recorded, imitating its structure.

SHARE your work.

Road Trip . . . . Geography

■ One of the marks of good fiction is that all references to the real world are precisely accurate. So . . .

IMAGINE that you are writing a novel.

WRITE a dialogue in which your main character is sitting in a cafe in a small town at the southern tip of Spain, overlooking the Strait of Gibraltar. Your character is telling the waiter about her (or his) trip here: She bought her motorcycle in Baku on the Caspian Sea, then rode to Turkey and along the Mediterranean coast to Spain. As you write her part of the dialogue, mention every country she passed through, and some cities. **EMBELLISH** the tale as much as you like, but remember to be accurate when referring to geography. **USE** the map on page 566 in the "Student Almanac" to help you. You may also want to consult other references.

Flash from the Past . . . . History

■ Flash fiction is very short fiction (from one paragraph to one page) written quickly. When you write flash fiction, you put a story on paper as it comes to you, structuring it "on the fly." Here's an exercise in writing flash fiction.

DO this minilesson with a partner.

Working separately, **CHOOSE** any three events listed in your handbook's time line.

LIST them on a sheet of paper.

TRADE lists with your partner.

Quickly **THINK** of a story or scenario that incorporates all three events.

WRITE DOWN your story in a flash.

Answer Key

Freeze-Dried Sentence (page 119)

Please respond to the Parent Teacher Association (in care of the district attorney) or the Better Business Bureau headquarters as soon as possible with miscellaneous literary illustrations about, for example, the gross national product of Russia, the intelligence quotients of very important persons, or the average miles per gallon of those with master of arts degrees in zoology.

In Praise of the Phrase (page 131)

1. studying a map
   to study a map
   studying a map

   > Studying a map is interesting.
   > I like to study a map.
   > Studying a map, we planned our trip.

2. taking a vacation
   to take a vacation
   taking a vacation

   > Taking a vacation is fun.
   > I like to take a vacation.
   > Taking a vacation, the family relaxed.

What a Circus! (page 131)

1. Simple
2. Complex
3. Compound-Complex
4. Compound-Complex
5. Compound

First, Last, and In Between (page 140)

The Lion in Winter

Clan of the Cave Bear

"By the Waters of Babylon"

Last Name, First Name (page 146)

Levenkron, Steven. Treating and Overcoming Anorexia Nervosa. New York: Charles Schribner's Sons, 1992.

Laurel, According to Hardy (page 147)

(Sentences will vary, but the parenthetical reference will not.)

. . . (qtd. in Zinsser 55).

If You Had To . . . (page 149)

John, where Jim had used just "had," had used "had had"; "had had" had had the teacher's approval.

Index